# SPELLCRAFT

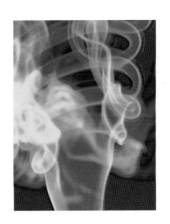

# SPELLCRAFT

## — a GRIMOIRE of —
## PRACTICAL MAGIC

Ann-Marie Gallagher

CARROLL & BROWN PUBLISHERS LIMITED

First published in 2001 in the United Kingdom by:

**CARROLL & BROWN PUBLISHERS LIMITED**
20 Lonsdale Road
Queen's Park
London NW6 6RD

**Editor**  Charlotte Beech
**Art Editor**  Gilda Pacitti
**Designer**  Roland Codd

**Photography**  David Murray and Jules Selmes

Text © 2001 Ann-Marie Gallagher
Illustration and compilation © 2001 Carroll & Brown

A CIP catalogue record for this book is available from the British Library.

ISBN 1-903258-21-9

Reproduced in Singapore by Colourscan
Printed and bound in Italy by Graphicom
First edition

# contents

# introduction

This book is based on the principle that magic is all around us, in the seas, the forests, and the crowded centres we call cities. It is not the reserve of a chosen few, but is accessible to anyone approaching it with respect and a down-to-earth attitude. Magic is so wonderful, it does not need rare and expensive ingredients, special courses or initiation into secret groups. It is part of our everyday world, and can be extraordinarily practical.

In order to do magic, or spellcraft, there is no need for the proverbial bat's blood, bubbling cauldron or hieroglyphics inscribed in blood on crumbling manuscripts. Neither will you have to set aside a room in your home to create a temple or paint pentagrams on the floor: you can cast spells anywhere in your home, or outside. Far from having to gather rare herbs and roots at an hour set by the ancient Babylonian calendar, you can get the ingredients for most of the spells from the kitchen, the office and the not-so-ancient supermarket.

## how spellcraft works

The type of magic used in this book is known as sympathetic magic, which has a venerable history and is recognized within many different cultures throughout the world. It works by using physical objects to represent your magical aims. For example, if you wish to diminish someone's harmful influence over you, you can use a thread to bind the petals of a flower representing their behaviour.

Resourcefulness and practicality are key to effective magic, so the spells in this book use everyday items as tools and ingredients. Therefore, even the common paperclip can be used in a spell to hold together a relationship and improve communications. You can also use objects to represent people. If you wish to implicate someone in particular, you can use a doll or a plasticine figure to embody him or her. All you have to do is to name the figure as that person at the beginning of the spell, and thus use the symbolic 'poppet' to bring about your wishes. To take an example, for a healing spell, you might submerge the doll in water, as water is associated with healing, see page 15. This does not mean, of course, that the person will drown! It is your intent, which finds expression through the symbols, that counts.

## setting your goals

Magic cannot solve all your problems, nor can it make you rich beyond your wildest dreams, but it can help you to achieve your realistic aims in life. Magic can be defined as 'that which connects'. Our relationships with other people, our work and the environment around us seem so ordinary that we rarely question them. In fact, the greatest magic of all is their very existence: although we cannot see physical lines joining people, places, thoughts and events, the links nonetheless exist. Using spells to project our will and encourage change to happen is actually a way of tapping into the wonderful web of connections that is magic. We trigger a reaction that travels the interlacing strands and reaches its destination in strange, and sometimes mysterious, ways.

You can use magic to help in most aspects of your life, and the spells in this book will cover many of the situations you are likely to encounter. Once you have practised some of these spells, you might like to try formulating some of your own – turn to pages 118–21 for advice on crafting your own spells. Remember always to be clear about what you want from a spell: if you are imprecise in what you ask for, you will get imprecise results.

## casting spells

The success of your magical work depends on when, where, and how you practise. Timing is all-important, and you will find advice on when best to perform a spell at the start of each one. The cycles of the Moon have a very powerful influence on magic, and specific phases of the Moon suit specific types of spell (see pages 42–3 for more information). The planets can also take a hand in the efficacy of spellwork. Each day of the week is ruled over by a different planet, so choosing the appropriate day to do magic can increase your success.

In theory you can cast a spell wherever you like, but in practise your choice will probably be dictated by the types of ingredients and tools you are using, and by the need for privacy. Unless otherwise stated, all spells in this book are designed to be performed on your own – your personal space (bedroom or study) is a good choice, though sometimes you may need to work in the kitchen, at your place of work or even outside (in which case you will need to pick a quiet spot).

## the magic circle

Many of the spells start by asking you to visualize a circle of light around you, your ingredients and the area in which you plan to work. The light represents the energy you are drawing through your body and forms a boundary to contain the power you will be raising, holding it there until it is ready to be released at the end of the spell. As you become accustomed to practising magic, you will notice the changes in energy that occur when you first cast your circle and when you have finished your work within it.

To cast your circle, you can either use a visualization on its own, or combine this visualization with the physical 'casting' of a circle and the lighting of candles to honour each of the five elements (see pages 12–17). For the latter, you will

need five candles. Set one in the east (to represent Air), one in the south (Fire), one in the west (Water), one in the north (Earth) and the last one in the centre (Spirit). Then cast your circle by visualizing a circle of white light encompassing the entire room or by directing your energy, visualized as white light, through your index finger to form a ring about your working space.

Beginning with Air, acknowledge the elements by standing before each candle saying: '**I call upon the element of** [Air/Fire/Water/Earth/Spirit]'. Light the candle appropriate to that element. When it is lit, honour the element by saying, '**Hail and welcome**'. Once you have honoured all the elements in this way, the circle is cast and sealed, and is ready for the spellwork to commence within.

## secrets of success

As well as timing, the types of ingredients and tools you use and the way that you use them can also influence the outcome of your spellwork. Colour, for example, is an important consideration. Each colour generates a different type of energy, affects your emotions in a certain way and has particular associations with the planets and the five elements. You can therefore use colour to enhance the power of your spells. You will find frequent recommendations as to the best colours to use (both in casting your magic and in choosing ingredients) in the spells given. When creating your own spells, refer to the tables of magical correspondences on pages 18 and 19 for advice.

Intoning carefully selected words and phrases as you perform a spell can also boost your chances of success. Using simple, straightforward words is one of the best ways of making clear your magical intentions. Again, plenty of examples are scattered through the pages of this book, some in rhyme, some not. Similarly, many spells recommend inscribing powerful symbols on your ingredients.

# aftercare

The 'Aftercare' section of each spell gives advice on consolidating your work. It tells you what you need to do with the main ingredients over the hours or months that follow your spell. On the whole, unless the candle is the main ingredient of the spell, it can simply be blown out and used again.

Items can be returned to their everyday use once the spell is completed, unless otherwise stated. The space in which you work can also be cleared and its normal function resumed just as soon as you have finished your work.

You may wish to find yourself a 'spellbox' – a container where you can keep items created in spellwork undisturbed until the spell's aim is accomplished. This can be made from any material you like, it is up to you whether you choose a traditional wooden box complete with lock, or a battered old ice-cream tub.

# ethics

There are traditional guidelines for the practice of magic, largely warning against irresponsibility. These include the so-called 'Law of threefold return', which holds that everything that you send out comes back to you in triplicate. This is often taken very literally to mean that a blessing or curse will be returned to you in kind, but three times more powerfully. Never having actually observed this, and being a practical sort of person, I would simply interpret this as a metaphor for taking responsibility for what you do.

You cannot cause harm accidentally by doing magic; it is your true intention that is carried. Nor can you directly affect the free will of another person by magic. It is not in the nature of magic that you can injure or save according to your will – this is not how it works. Magic works with nature, not against it. Taking responsibility for your magical actions involves working out what is really

required; what needs to be drawn or attracted, what needs to be banished or sent away. Each situation has to be analysed on its own terms. So if someone approaches you to perform a specific spell, listen hard to what he or she has to say before assessing whether that spell is suitable. For example, if a friend tells you she is being victimized at work and asks you to cast a spell to help her transfer to another post, think carefully whether this is the most appropriate course of action. Perhaps she is simply suffering from a lack of confidence, and a spell to boost her self-worth would be of more use. However, if there is some genuine victimization involved, take appropriate action—be it magical or official.

Taking responsibility in magic is a vital part of the whole process. Spellcraft is primarily designed to spread positive and peaceful intentions – use it as such and you'll reap the benefits!

## how to use this book

The spells have been divided into six chapters that relate to major aspects of your life: career; love; health; home; family, friends and neighbours; and prosperity. Scattered throughout these pages you will also find a few red disks. These hide special information on how to boost the effectiveness of the spell in question. The only way to make these hints and tips appear is by covering them with the specially provided bookmark.

You will also find numerous special features scattered throughout this book, which expand upon some of the other issues, ingredients and considerations of spellcraft. These include the importance of the Moon's phases, the role of needlework in magic, the use of everyday objects in magic, building a magical home and the role of banishing and binding spells.

# the 5 magical elements

The framework of the five elements used in this book is very common in the magical systems of Europe, including Britain and Ireland, and North America. Originally set down in writing over 2000 years ago by the Greeks, this formula was offered as a theory explaining the composition of everything in existence.

In magic, each of the elements is associated with a different type of concern: Air with communication, Fire with energy, Water with emotions, Earth with matter and Spirit with connection. Of course, there are many subtleties of representation within each category, but this division of labour is very useful. It enables us to construct spells and channel our intentions through the use of a basic system of symbols. The five elements also have a number of correspondences, including colours, planets, images and other representations, all of which can be employed in practical spellwork.

In the physical world, four of the elements can be experienced in their purest forms as the air that we breathe, water we drink, fire that we cook with and earth that we walk upon. Spirit is the glue that binds all these together, and though it cannot be experienced as literally as its fellows, its role as the connective element can be said to directly influence the form of all things in existence.

As you work with magic more and more, you will get to know the different and subtle aspects of the elements. You will, most likely, find yourself exploring or meditating upon the meaning of the each one. If you use magic frequently as a part of everyday life, you may also consider honouring them as an integral part of casting a magical circle (see pages 8–9).

# air

Air is the first element we encounter at birth when we take our opening breath as individual human beings. That all-important breath enables us to pass from one stage of life, growth in the womb, to another, growth outside it. Perhaps reflecting the part air plays at the beginning of our lives, its elemental form oversees travel and communications.

In more formal magical circles, Air is traditionally the first element to be honoured. Associated with the planet Mercury, it represents swiftness, mental agility and the ability to transform ideas into actions. Meditations upon the element of Air, in all its physical and symbolic aspects, are useful in promoting clarity, perspective and enhancing one's ability to speak and write articulately. Air tends to act as a facilitator in magic, and is useful in spells concerned with examinations, travel, vehicles, commerce, writing, publishing and legal matters. Wherever there is a blockage in communication, Air is the ideal element to draw upon.

In the cycle of the day, Air is connected with the dawn, and, as such, is generally placed in the east of a circle – the direction of sunrise. It is also associated with Spring and new birth in the wheel of the year, and the colour symbolizing Air is yellow – the colour of daffodils and egg yolks.

Aquarius, Gemini and Libra are all Air signs, and those born under them are said to be especially articulate and communicative.

# fire

Fire exists physically in many forms. In more developed societies, it takes the form of energy transmitted through electricity and solar power. Within ourselves, it is the spark that leaps from synapse to synapse, and is the warmth of our bodies, which have to stay above a certain temperature to function and survive. It is also the Sun, star-parent of this planet and provider of the energy needed for life on Earth. In the magical circle, Fire is usually the second element to be welcomed.

In magical terms, Fire is associated with action, courage and inspiration. It is seen as an energizing force, representing enthusiasm, belief and willpower, and it gives the ability to face adversity. It is also seen as a purifying force – for example, in its manifestation as lightning and spontaneous combustion after drought, it has been known to start forest fires, which function to clear forests and enable new life to spring up from the soil. Fire is best used in spells for courage, inspiration or willpower. It is ideal to inspire enthusiasm, to help galvanize someone into action or to move forwards decisively.

The time of day associated with Fire is noon, when the sun is at its height. Summer is the season of Fire, and in magical circles it is traditionally placed in the south, where hotter lands lie (providing you live north of the equator). It is symbolized by the colour red.

The astrological Fire signs are Aries, Leo and Sagittarius, and Fire people are reputedly energetic, fiery and inspirational.

# water

Water is our home before we are born. Floating in the womb, we develop and grow, waiting to join the outside world. The theory of human evolution also holds that all life started in the great oceans of the Earth millions of years ago – so water is key to how humans and other animals came into being in the first place.

Physically, water is present in the fluids of the human body, which is itself composed of up to 80 per cent water. Tears, milk and menstrual blood are linked to the emotions, to nourishment and to women's reproductive cycles. It is hardly surprising, then, that in magic, Water is connected with love, healing and the cycles of the Moon. Perhaps on account of the time we spend floating in the fluids of our mother's womb, a time which we do not yet fully understand, Water is also associated with dreaming and the psychic powers of the mind. This element is wonderful for spells that are to do with healing, love, psychic powers, dreams and balance. Water's ability to always find its own level also makes it ideal for matters of natural justice.

Water is associated with the sunset, as well as autumn. In traditional magical circles, this element is placed at the west, the place of the sunset, and it is most often symbolized by the colour blue.

The Water signs of the zodiac are Pisces, Cancer and Scorpio. People born under these signs are supposed to be emotional, sensitive and deep.

# earth

Earth is the name of the planet on which we stand, and its presence is found within, below and around us. The element of Earth can be seen in our chemical composition: in the trace minerals, such as iron and magnesium, which our bodies need, and in the calcium and protein of our nails, teeth, bones and hair.

In magic, Earth is associated with manifestation, and its gift is the physical world. Whereas Water is connected with fertility through its affiliation with women's cycles, Earth is the element that sees potentiality through to fruition. We often refer to soil and compost as 'earth' and this is where food and other necessities take root and grow. When the growth is completed, we harvest the crops and eat or sell them. Accordingly, the magical associations of Earth are wealth, shelter, sufficiency, property, material need and physical health. Spellwork focusing on housing, material, money issues, work for the environment and physical well-being are best done under the auspices of this element.

In circles created for magical purposes, Earth is traditionally placed in the north. Perhaps because the Sun's disc is seen to sink below the Earth's surface at night, Earth is linked with midnight. It is symbolized by the colour green, which itself is associated with trees and plant life growing on the planet.

Capricorn, Taurus and Virgo are all Earth signs. People born under them are allegedly good with money, slightly materialistic and very practical.

# spirit

Spirit is affiliated with connection and transformation. Sometimes referred to as 'the fifth element' or as 'Ether', it is perhaps the least obvious of the elements to pin down. As it represents connection between all things, it does not have a physical presence of its own. In a traditional magical circle, Spirit is either not symbolized at all, on the grounds that its presence is obvious, or is given central place and represented by a purple or white candle.

Its symbol is the web, the archetypal image of interconnection. When we think of the physical construction of a web we tend not to be as interested by the substance from which it is spun as we are by the way it is linked together. Webs generally become visible to the human eye only when something is moving or is caught on it, whether a spider, a prey or the raindrops left after a heavy mist. This is similar to the way in which Spirit functions; it is often perceived only when it gives shape or substance to something else.

In magic, the spokes of the Spirit web are seen as the different stages of human life, or the changing of the seasons. The spiral of the Spirit web is seen as the never-ending cycle of life and death. Accordingly, this element is invoked to help in spells to do with transformation, change, and spirituality. It is recommended for rituals of spiritual growth and knowledge, and blessings for those taking the path of magic.

# the days of the week

| DAY | PLANETARY CORRESPONDENCE | COLOUR | CHARACTERISTICS | SPELL EXAMPLES |
|---|---|---|---|---|
| SUNDAY | the Sun | gold, yellow | health, success, happiness | for general success and well-being |
| MONDAY | the Moon | silver, white | the tides, women's menstrual cycles, dreams, mental health | for women's health, money, mental stability and in prophecy |
| TUESDAY | Mars | red | courage, fieriness, will, inspiration, laughter, community | for protection, bravery, stimulation and to draw friends |
| WEDNESDAY | Mercury | yellow | communications, speed, commerce, mental agility, memory, travel, the law | for moving on, exams, communication, vehicles and in legal matters |
| THURSDAY | Jupiter | purple, deep blue | generosity, expansiveness, pleasure, property issues, justice, sacrifice, luck | for good luck, increase, fairness and matters of property |
| FRIDAY | Venus | green | love, friendship, beauty, harmony, peace | for finding love, friends, balance and a sense of personal peace |
| SATURDAY | Saturn | black or brown | restriction, discipline, banishment, binding | for binding and banishing bad behaviour and for giving up bad habits |

# the table of correspondences

| ELEMENT | AIR | FIRE | WATER | EARTH | SPIRIT |
|---|---|---|---|---|---|
| | | | | | |
| COLOUR | yellow | red | blue | green | purple/white |
| TREES | pine, birch, sycamore | oak, juniper | apple, willow, chestnut | yew, cypress | ash |
| OILS AND INCENSES | pine, citronella, citrus fruits, lavender, eucalyptus | frankincense, rosemary | rose, geranium, apple, poppy, black pepper, cinnamon | patchouli, lily sandalwood, ylang-ylang, jasmine, cedar | sage, thyme, cypress, marjoram |
| TIME OF DAY/YEAR | dawn/spring | noon/summer | sunset/autumn | midnight/winter | |
| CHARACTERISTICS | communication, ideas, memory, education | courage, will, inspiration, purification | love, healing, natural justice, dreams, Moon power | manifestation, the material world, fertility, tides | connection, knowledge, magical stability |
| SPELL TYPES | exams, tests, travel and vehicles, writing and speech, commerce, legal matters | courage, inspiration, willpower, encouragement, facing adversity | love, friendship, healing, need, emotional balance, natural justice, psychic power | houses/property, money, material need, protection, well-being, physical health, crops | spiritual growth, magic, psychic abilities, blessings |
| TRADITIONAL TOOLS/PRACTICAL TOOLS | wand/broom, office equipment, wineglass | dagger (athame) /kitchen knife or penknife | chalice or cauldron/coffee or tea cup, the Internet | pentagram/ dinner plate, bread board | pentacle, web or spiral/ quartz crystal |
| GIFTS | music, poetry, writing, thinking | dance, enthusiasm, acting on belief | gentleness, patience, love and affection | health, material blessings, loyalty, stability | magic, awareness, ability to see beyond appearances |
| COMPASS POINT | east | south | west | north | |

19

# ① career

The spells in this chapter all relate to your career or working life – whether this involves enabling you to articulate or demonstrate your abilities, gain recognition, move into a new career path or improve your working environment.

The terms career, work and study should all be taken in their broadest senses. Career and work can be applied as meaningfully to an academic path, voluntary work or household management as they can to office work. Study can also be understood as all forms of learning, not just the pursuit of a formal qualification.

Of course, all spells must be based on realistic expectations – nothing in the world short of cheating or advances in telepathy is going to get you through an interview or exam for which you are not prepared! Spellcraft does, however, give you a new means of thinking about your aims and ambitions, perhaps in ways you've never considered before, and getting to grips with your own professional identity – that of your everyday work – is a vital part of this process.

# for a new job, promotion or success in an exam

This is best carried out on a waxing Moon, as you are drawing success towards you. Wednesday, day of Mercury, the planet of communications, is ideal.

This spell is both versatile and adaptable. Getting a new job, winning promotion or seeking success in an exam all have at least three things in common: they are all different means of communicating your abilities, they are all related to gaining recognition for your endeavours, and they are all related to your career potential. The same spell, therefore, can be used for any of these purposes.

As with all magic, asking for miracles inevitably ends in disappointment, so your wishes should be based on the firm foundation of possibility. Sitting an exam without revising or applying for a job or promotion for which you are not qualified is unlikely to yield the desired result.

**You will need...**
3–4 tbsp water
1 oil burner
A few drops essential oil (pine, cinnamon or vanilla) or 1 pinch of powdered cinnamon
1 tea light
1 yellow candle
1 nail, sewing needle or pin

# yellow candle spell

Ensure that you can work in a private, undisturbed space and that there is a safe place to let your candle burn down completely – this may take several hours so you will need to put it where it will be attended at all times. You could cut a long candle down to size to minimize the burning-down time, but ensure that you will have enough room to scratch the required words and symbols into the wax.

Visualize a circle of yellow light all around you, your gathered ingredients and the space in which you will be working.

Pour water into the dish of the oil burner and add either the specified essential oil or a pinch of powdered cinnamon. Light a tea light inside the burner.

Hold up your yellow candle with both hands and visualize yourself opening an envelope containing good exam results, a job offer or news of a promotion. When you have finished seeing yourself achieve your goal, hold the candle close to your mouth and say firmly three times: **'I charge this candle to contain my wish, which is to** [wish]**'.**

Take the nail, needle or pin and carve into the side of the candle, running from bottom to top (wick end), your first name, one word that represents your wish and the symbol of the planet Mercury (see above).

Light the candle, saying: **'As this candle burns away, may my wish be released to become reality: So mote it be'.**

**Aftercare** Allow the candle to burn completely away; do not allow it to go out until it reaches the very end of the candle. It does not need to remain in the space where you lit it, but should be kept in sight for safety's sake.

# to stop bullying

As with all diminishing spells, this is best carried out on a waning Moon. Saturday (day of the disciplinary, restrictive planet Saturn) is best, but may not be practical if you have to use the photocopier at work. If this is the case, any day will do – it is, after all, the intent that matters.

This spell marries the age-old principles of sympathetic magic with modern technology, and is particularly effective if carried out by the person being bullied. You may, however, do this for someone else.

As you are going to name and banish someone's harmful influence, you will need to replace it with something positive to ensure that the old pattern of negative conduct is not simply replaced by similar bad habits. In the case of an abusive co-worker, for example, a good replacement would be: respect for the rights or feelings of others. That is the gift you send to your colleague, and by extension to all people with whom he or she has contact. The best way to find a replacement is to think about why you are banishing the influence or behaviour in question, and to focus on the overall purpose of the spell.

Whether you perform this spell at home or at work, make sure that you do it in private and that you are not disturbed for the duration of the spell.

**You will need...**
1 photograph or image of, or signature or piece of writing from, the person whose influence or power you wish to reduce or eradicate
1 photocopier
Several blank sheets of paper
1 recycle bin

# photocopier spell

Stand by the photocopier, and visualize a white circle of light all around you, the machine and the recycle bin.

Holding the image or writing, name it as the person whose influence and power you are seeking to diminish, saying aloud: **'I name you** [person]**'**.

Place it on the photocopier, ready to be copied. Adjust the darkness control to its lightest setting. Then, as you press the button to copy, say: **'...and thus I reduce your power to harm'**.

Now take the lightened copy and photocopy this as above, reciting the same words. Place the original image or writing in the bin. Continue copying the lightened sheets and recycling the one just copied, until the image is completely faded and only blank paper comes out.

Hold this blank page, saying aloud: **'Just as I wipe out your imprint, so shall your harmful influence cease to be. I replace it with** [name the replacement]**'**.

Write the replacement on the page and fold it, saying: **'So mote it be'**.

**Aftercare**   Keep the folded paper in a safe place until the thing you have willed has come to be. At the next waxing Moon, cast a circle and light a candle to celebrate the success of the spell. Burn the paper over the candle flame, saying: **'As this fire transforms paper to ash, so magic has turned harm to good that it may not be undone'**. Use the ashes in your garden to continue the positive transformation, and grow something wonderful in the soil.

# binding and banishing

The word 'binding' is a metaphor meaning 'to tie up'. A binding spell prevents wrongdoers from continuing in their harmful actions. It works by binding a symbol of the person involved with cords to symbolize their damaging behaviour. They will then find themselves hampered in all areas of life until they stop behaving badly. In this way, the wrongdoer is literally bound by their own behaviour.

Banishing spells work by sending away the origin of the harm – for example, a person's rude or thoughtless behaviour. There are various ways of symbolizing a banishing. One way is to mould a wax figure to embody the behaviour you wish to get rid of and then to melt it. Another method would be to use plasticine to adapt the shape of an ice tray in order to make an ice shape exemplifying what you wish to banish. It can then be defrosted in a microwave.

## restoring the balance

When you are banishing, you must always replace. The basic rule is to name, banish and then replace. This is to ensure that bad behaviour is not simply succeeded by something worse. Changing the pattern from a negative to a positive one is a responsibility you take on when you decide to banish. What you use to replace the thing you have excised should be appropriate to the situation. For example, if you are seeking to banish someone's selfish behaviour, the gift of consideration for others would be a suitable replacement.

## working your magic

Traditionally, all bindings and banishings take place on a waning or dark (new) Moon. Since these spells are a means of diminishing or taking power away – in this case, the power to do harm – they work best as the Moon is diminishing or has disappeared from sight.

These spells are suitable to a number of situations. Sometimes, for example, we inadvertently do harm to ourselves by hanging onto sad memories, regrets or past relationships. In such cases, you can use the principles of either banishing or binding to ritually cut away the feelings of attachment. Binding is useful where you wish to put aside troublesome feelings or bad memories until you are ready to face them and deal with them.

One of the most common worries attached to banishing and binding spells is the fear that by using them, you are effectively 'cursing' someone. This is simply not so – in banishing harmful behaviour or binding a troublemaker you are working to prevent harm being done. The only worry that might possibly arise from using these charms is the temptation to invest all your efforts in a spell rather than take practical action first. As always, magic is not a substitute for, but a companion to, common sense.

# to promote harmony at work or school

To be carried out early in the cycle of the waxing Moon, as you are planting the seeds of harmony, which will reach full growth in due course. Best undertaken on a Friday, day of the harmonious planet Venus.

This spell is designed for people who use e-mail. It combines modern technology with the ancient wisdom of the runes, one of which is found on your keyboard in the shape of the letter 'x'. This is the rune 'gifu', which means 'gift'. Interestingly, people signing cards or gift-tags often write kisses using this symbol. This modern usage of the rune is extended to mean 'harmony' rather than 'love' and is sent as a gift to your office- or schoolmates, some of whom may not be especially lovable!

Attaining an atmosphere of harmony is also, of course, a gift to yourself. All workplaces and schools can be hot houses of stress, anxiety and subsequently interpersonal tensions. Since we spend most of our week-day hours there, it is reasonable to want the atmosphere to be pleasant and supportive. This spell quietly distributes the gift of harmony via e-mail, thus using something that can itself be a source of tension in these modern times.

**You will need...**
1 workstation, linked to e-mail
1 e-mail address-list of all co-workers in your immediate work environment

# e-mail spell

Perform this spell in your workplace or school. Although you will not require privacy, you will need to concentrate for the duration of the spell. Do this when you next have occasion to send an e-mail to all of your co-workers at the same time. If such an occasion doesn't arise when you need it to, invent one!

Visualize a circle of pale blue light surrounding your workspace. Log onto your e-mail.

Selecting the appropriate addressees, concentrate in turn on each person in your workplace, visualizing them at work – smiling, helpful and polite.

Type out your memo, and when you have finished press the space-bar on your keyboard three times, write your name and press the space-bar another three times.

Take the cursor to the centre of the page, and concentrate on your vision of a peaceful and happy office. Say out loud, or silently if appropriate: **'Three gifts I give, For three times three, I send you peace, And harmony'.**

Hit the 'x' key three times, leaving a print on the screen that looks like this: **xxx**.

Send the e-mail.

> **Aftercare** Having sent a threefold 'gifu' to your workmates, you will need a ready-made excuse in case anyone spots them and asks why you're sending 'kisses'. A simple 'Did I? How odd!' is better than lying or telling them you have cast a spell. Lying would undermine this spell, while revelations of spell-casting may earn you more personal space than you bargained for.

# to get your ideas heard by others

To be carried out on a waxing Moon. Wednesday, the day of Mercury, messenger of the gods, is best for this spell.

Whether you are a student, a worker or participating in a neighbourhood committee, it can be extremely frustrating to be ignored when you are trying to be heard. Perhaps you are a quiet person, not used to being assertive, or it could be that your colleagues aren't particularly cooperative or used to listening to other peoples' views. Either way, this spell is great for evening out those difficulties that prevent you communicating your ideas effectively.

Bubbles are a particularly good medium for 'getting the message across' magically. They contain and float upon air, which is the appropriate element to work with in matters of communication, whether spoken or written. In this case, the bubbles will quite literally carry your message.

Of course, if you feel that it is your communication skills that need strengthening, you can use this spell in a more general sense towards that end, and support this by looking out for assertiveness or public-speaking classes.

**You will need...**
- 1 yellow or white candle, or tea light
- 1 incense stick (any scent) and holder
- 1 bottle of children's 'bubble' liquid complete with bubble hoop (available from most toy shops)

# bubble spell

You will need complete privacy for this spell, whether you carry it out at home or in the place where you are having trouble getting heard. Otherwise, not only will the spell be interrupted or literally 'broken', but you will also get a reputation for eccentricity!

Visualize a circle of yellow light all around you, your gathered ingredients and the space in which you will be working.

Light the candle and the incense stick in the centre of your circle of light. Then take the incense and, ensuring it is secure in the holder, carry it around your working space clockwise before returning it to the centre.

Concentrating on the candle flame, say aloud: **'I call upon the powers of Air to witness and aid me in my wish to be heard'.**

Dipping the bubble hoop in the mixture, blow a bubble by speaking one word at a time of the following sentence into a bubble, and letting each bubble float and burst at will: **'May my ideas fly out like birds, That all will stop to hear my words'.**

**Aftercare** Now that your words have been carried in the bubbles, which eventually burst and release your wishes to go and do their work, all you have to do is await the results.

# to get a raise in salary

If you can, perform this spell on a waxing Moon, as you are asking for increase. Sunday, day of the Sun, which presides over success in business, is ideal.

If you are not a particularly gifted cook you will be delighted to learn that this spell is designed especially for the hard-of-baking. Not only does it save you the effort and expense of purchasing separate ingredients for cake making by using an instant mix – it also uses an electric whisk so that you can save your energy to apply for that raise. This spell uses the principle of sympathetic magic by equating the 'raise' you are looking for with the 'rising' of the cake in the oven. Because it is always nice to share your good fortune, this cake should be distributed amongst your co-workers, so resist the temptation to nibble once it is out of the oven!

# cake spell

You will need the kitchen to yourself for about forty minutes. You should avoid making any loud noises when the cake is in the oven, as this will prevent it from rising. Be careful to follow the instructions on the cake-mix packet in order to stop the cake, and thereby your spell, from falling flat.

Visualize a circle of golden light all around the kitchen, and light the candle, saying: **'I call upon the energies of the sun to witness and bless my wish for a raise in my salary'.**

Place the cake mixture, egg(s) and water or milk in a bowl and prepare to whisk.

While you are whisking with an electric beater for the requisite amount of time, visualize yourself reading your bank statement and seeing a higher figure for the salary paid into your account and chant the following until the mixture is ready: **'By the mixing of this spell, See my worth and pay me well'.**

When the mixture is ready, place the foil-covered coin in one of the tins, divide the cake mixture in two and pour it evenly into both.

Place the mixture into a pre-heated oven, at the temperature and for the length of time specified on the packet. As you shut the oven door, say: **'As you rise, may my fortunes rise with you'.**

When the sponges are ready, remove from the oven. Removing the coin, spread each sponge with jam and, when cool, join the pieces together to make a 'jam sandwich'.

**Aftercare** Firstly, make sure that no one in your home eats the cake! Take it to work with you the next day and enjoy it with your co-workers.

# for change or moving on

This is best cast on a waxing Moon, for progress and increase, and if possible, on a Tuesday, day of the feisty planet Mars. Although Mercury generally represents commerce, communication and transitions, Mars holds the galvanizing action vibes needed to get things moving.

It can be difficult to decide how and when to make changes to your working life. Sometimes, even if you have made your mind up to go, the move from one phase of your career to another can be fraught, especially if you have been in one job for a long time.

If you have reached one of those sticky moments when you know you need a change but cannot see how to achieve it, or simply feel hampered in your progress, this spell is ideal. It focuses on your individual progress from one situation to another by taking the symbol of a paper doll and literally moving a representation of you into a different place.

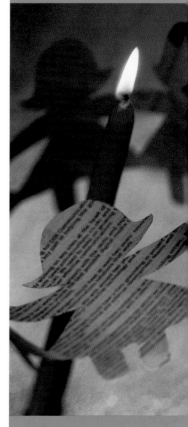

**You will need...**
1 red candle
1 sheet of paper from the careers section of a newspaper, cut to approximately 60 x 10 cm
1 pen, black ink
1 pair of scissors
2 small lengths of sticky tape

# paper doll spell

You may need to practise making paper dolls before proceeding if you are unfamiliar with the process.

Light the red candle and call upon the dynamism and fire-power of Mars saying: **'May I be granted energy for the changes I now face'**.

Fold the paper into a concertina form of six 10 x 10-cm squares.

Take the pen and draw the outline of yourself on the front of the paper, taking care to ensure that the hands and feet of the doll continue into the folds. Cut out the shapes using the scissors, ensuring that the links across the folds are not cut or damaged. Unfold, so that you have a continuous chain of six paper dolls, joined together by hands and feet.

Write your name and the words **'Where I am now'** on the doll to the far left and your name and the words **'Where I want to be'** on the doll to the far right.

Visualizing yourself leaving your present job and entering another place of work, and smiling, fold the dolls back up and fasten shut with the two pieces of sticky tape, saying: **'From where I am to where I'll be, Increase the opportunity'**.

**Aftercare** Keep your paper dolls in a safe place until you have achieved the desired move, then discard in the waste recycle bin.

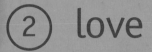

# ② love

One of the most asked-for types of spell is for love, but there are almost as many forms of love spell as there are kinds of love.

One way of bringing a little warmth and affection into your life is to make yourself ready for it. This may mean getting to know and appreciate yourself or building your self-confidence. Then you will be ready to send out a message that the time is right for love to come to you. If you simply want to attract attention and have some fun, you can cast a spell to this effect – provided you are honest with yourself and those you attract.

Not all love spells are about attracting new partners – some are good for reinforcing an established relationship, or for moving on when it is over. You can use these spells to enhance communications in a loving relationship, inject a little extra passion, help your partner appreciate him- or herself or diminish the hurt of a rocky episode. You can also bless another couple, a worthy objective for a love spell. And last, but not least, these spells can help you to think about, recognize and address your own emotional needs.

# for love to come into your life

To be enacted on a waxing Moon, as you are drawing love towards you, and when the tide is out. Friday, the day of the love planet Venus, is the ideal day on which to cast.

**You will need...**
1 sandy beach by the sea, a tidal river or estuary
1 stick or long, thin pebble, preferably found on a beach

This spell is particularly suited to situations where the supplicant is ready for a new relationship to come into his or her life. As the element most associated with love is water, this spell is best cast on a beach or next to a tidal river. Here, the tides are used to symbolize the changes of your emotional life. Because this spell does not name a specific person to come to you, it may give the impression of being somewhat 'wishy-washy'. In fact, it is all the more powerful for being so! Because it is very specific about the wish for love or 'a worthy lover', and because it is the wash of water that carries that wish out on the tide, it is both 'wishy' and 'washy'. Recognition of the ebb and flow of your life-tides, implied by choosing to cast this spell, is an integral part of powerful magic.

# seaside spell

As beaches and shorelines are public space, you may not get complete privacy for the duration of your spell. This is fine, but you will need to concentrate and may need to adjust your 'chant' for public consumption.

Take your stick and inscribe a circle in the sand all around you to a diameter of approximately two metres.

Draw an overlapping circle to the side of the first circle so that the interlinked circles are parallel to the water line. Stay within these circles until you have finished your part in the spell.

In the left-hand circle (facing inshore), inscribe your name leaving out all vowels and drawing the consonants each on top of the other. To the right, in the same circle, draw an inverted triangle, the symbol of water (see above).

Stepping into the right-hand circle, draw a picture of something beautiful associated with water, as a gift to the sea. Be creative!

Standing in the space where the circles overlap, chant or sing something appropriate, for example, **'Grandmother ocean, carry my spell'**, to the incoming tide. Repeat your chant at least nine times.

Say aloud to the sea or river: **'I ask for love to come into my life. Take my wish, incoming tide, and carry it out when you turn again. May this wish be granted on the next incoming tide of my life. So mote it be'**.

**Aftercare** Since the sea washes away your drawings, all you need to do is wait for a new lover to arrive when the time is right.

# to attract a prospective lover

Cast this enchantment on a waxing Moon, as you are seeking to attract something to you. Friday, presided over by Venus, the love and passion planet, is best.

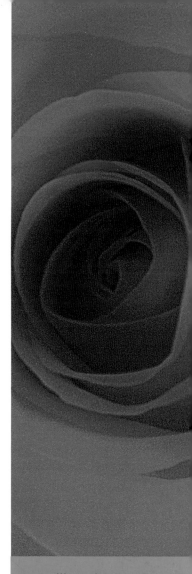

This, as with all love spells in this book, is not directed at the object of your desire, but at you. The enchantment works by attracting the desired sexual or romantic interest of others. Although it is not necessarily aimed at bringing the love of your life to you, it is certainly a bonus when this does happen!

An open honey-pot can bring all sorts of flying insects buzzing around – some of them with stings. Take care to attract only the right sort of person to you by being very clear during the visualization part of this spell about the type of lover you need. You will notice that the spell ends with the words: 'And harm come to none'. This is to underline your intent that any liaison ensuing from this spell will be good for both you and your new lover.

**You will need...**
1 candle – red for passion or pink for romance
1 rosebud, or any other attractive flower bud
A few drops of water
1 jar of clear honey, with a lid

# honey jar spell

The flower bud will be representing you, so be sure to choose an attractive one!

Light your chosen candle saying: **'I call upon Aphrodite, goddess of love, to witness and bless my spell'.**

Hold the flower bud in your left hand and with your right, sprinkle it with drops of water, saying as appropriate: **'I name this flower as my romantic attraction, and freshen it so'.**

Remove the lid of the honey jar, and hold it in both hands. Gaze into the honey, and visualizing situations in which you might find yourself with a new lover, sing to the honey. This can be a simple chant where you make up the words and tune, for example, **'My love is sweet as honey, honey to the bee'**, or a popular song that you feel is appropriate.

While you are still singing or chanting, take the flower bud and press it into the honey, saying: **'May the sweetness of this honey attract a new lover to me'.**

Replace the lid firmly, saying: **'And harm come to none'.**

**Aftercare** Blow out the candle and relight it in your bedroom each night to burn for an hour after sunset, until it burns out. Keep the honey jar, with the flower bud still within it, under your bed for one moon cycle. Then, if your dietary requirements allow it, you should eat the honey yourself until the jar is empty. This may take some time if you take a little each day, so ensure that no one else in the household dips in. Your new lover should appear before you finish the honey.

# the tides of the Moon

The Moon, our nearest celestial neighbour, has long fascinated earthlings. The shapes seen on its surface have been likened to many forms, including a rabbit, a baby and a human face. In many mythologies, the Moon, as it shines in the night as the Sun shines in the day, has been portrayed as the sister, brother, wife or husband of the Sun, and various gods and goddesses have lunar associations.

## the lunar phases

The word month actually comes from the word Moon and means one lunar cycle. Actually, all calendar months apart from February have either 30 or 31 days, which is rather more than the 27⅓ days it takes for the Moon to revolve around the earth. During this cycle, because it shines by reflected sunlight, it displays different phases – from new to crescent, half, gibbous, full and slowly diminishing down to new again. In magic, the new phase is often called Dark Moon. At this point the disc of the Moon reflects no light at all.

In accordance with the principles of sympathetic magic, each phase of the Moon is considered suitable for different magical purposes. The Dark Moon is traditionally a time for endings, so is suitable for banishing, binding and exorcism. The waxing phase – from the day after Dark Moon to the day before full Moon, is the time for attracting and drawing in, for increase and growth. The full Moon is associated with witches coming together to work magic –

but most witches use this time to celebrate their spirituality and save spell work for when the Moon is growing or diminishing. The waning phase, from the day after full Moon and up to and including Dark Moon, is used to send things away, reduce or diminish.

This is only a general guide – some spells are best cast early in a waxing Moon, others in the last half Moon. But the principle is sound – waxing Moon equals increase, and waning decrease. On pages 124–25 you'll find a calendar charting all the Moon's phases.

## how the Moon affects us

The association between the Moon's phases and different types of magic is not arbitrary. Its relationship with Earth is of a real and physical nature. Its pull affects our oceans, causing tides. Gardeners swear by planting seed at Dark Moon, and research shows that the lunar cycle does indeed affect plant life. Shipwrights once refused to fell trees during a waxing Moon, claiming that only wood felled in the second quarter of a waning Moon dried quickly enough.

There also have been strong associations made between lunar and reproductive cycles throughout history, and the average cycle does indeed correlate roughly to the length of one lunar revolution. This similarity led to the Moon being associated with menstruation, pregnancy and childbirth. Accordingly, in magic, it presides over the life cycle, covering birth, fertility and death.

# to promote communication between partners

This spell should be cast on a waxing Moon as it seeks to encourage openness and healthy communication. Love spells are generally cast on Friday, the day of Venus. However, this spell emphasizes conversation, so Wednesday is best.

This is a lovely spell, which is suitable not only for when there are problems within a relationship, but also to ensure the continuation of good communications between a couple. In the case of the latter, you may wish to cast this spell as a gift to friends who are getting together – after seeking their approval, of course! It works just as well for you and your partner, however.

The use of paperclips in a love spell may seem unusual to those more inclined to associate love with hearts and roses. However, the more practical may recognize that one of the most important aspects of strong and long-lasting relationships is good communication. Paperclips are a wonderful symbol of togetherness; after all, they are used in offices the world over to keep things together in transit!

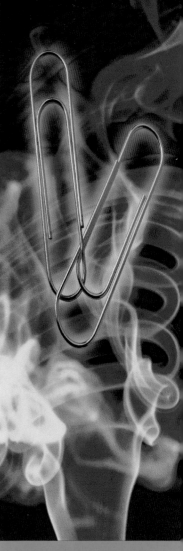

**You will need...**
- 1 incense stick – any scent – and holder
- 1 ballpoint pen with black or blue ink
- 2 plain office paperclips
- 1 plain envelope
- 1 plain hand-mirror
- 1 postage stamp

# paperclip spell

Although the scent of the incense needn't be specific, it would be nice, if possible, to use a love-related incense such as romantic rose or sexy sandalwood. The hand-mirror should be placed on the floor at the centre of your workspace, reflecting side up.

Light the incense stick and cast your workspace by carrying it around the room clockwise.

Take the pen and write the names and address of the couple in question on the envelope.

Taking a paperclip in each hand, pass them both through the incense smoke three times before placing them on the mirror, saying as you do: **'Bless, by this smoke** [name of first person] **on my left and** [name of other person] **on my right, May you pass through no other cloud but sweetness and travel in light'.**

Hold up the mirror, breathe onto the paperclips so that the glass is misted, and the outline of the paperclips is left on the mirror. Remove paperclips and place to one side.

Lifting the mirror aloft, say out loud: **'May nothing cloud your judgement in your dealings with each other'.** Replace the mirror on the floor.

Take the paperclips and link them together, saying: **'I wish you clarity and good communications'.** Place the linked paperclips in the envelope and seal it. Stick the postage stamp to it with a firm, **'So mote it be!'**

**Aftercare** Post the letter as soon as possible after the spell. The paperclips should be kept somewhere safe by the named couple as a charm for good communications thereafter.

# using everyday objects

Because this is a practical spell book, you will find most of the
ingredients and tools in your kitchen, office, shed or in your local
shopping centre. Sometimes, however, you will need to substitute
an ingredient or tool that you do not have to hand. Alternatively,
inspired by the ideas in this book and the guidance on sympathetic
magic, you may consider putting together spells of your own.

## modern-day magic

Office equipment and modern technology provide a wealth of tools
and symbols for use in magic. Paperclips can be used to unite
couples, families or friends in harmony. Staplers can be used for
joining spells, whilst hole-punches used on rice paper can create
word confetti for sprinkling wishes onto a party cake. Screensavers
on computers are ideal for running chants, affirmations or verbal
charms of protection. Used imaginatively, the contrast function on a
photocopier can either fade or embolden a symbolic image, plus
creative use of your e-mail filter will enable you to bounce back
abusive mail, and thereby its bad vibes, to anyone harassing you.

Kitchen equipment is endlessly versatile. It is possible, for
instance, to symbolize the five elements from the contents of your
cupboards: for Air, a whisk; for Fire, an ordinary kitchen knife; for
Water, a cup; for Earth, a breadboard; and for Spirit, a web or cat's
cradle made from string. The stove is ideal for melting wax or ice

symbols, baking magical cakes and burning effigies, while the ice-box is great for freezing symbolic shapes, or leaving items for binding spells. The herb and spice rack offers endless possibilities – spices can be used to 'heat up' love spells, and berries and herbs to make easy, cheap and effective incenses.

## hands-on materials

DIY enthusiasts are probably unaware of the magical potential contained in the average garage, shed or toolbox. Blowtorches, used with safety in mind, are brilliant accessories for magically 'blasting' obstacles, melting wax or ice figures and obliterating symbols of harm. Vices and workbenches are great in spells for courage, steadfastness or binding. Electric drills are great for facilitating communications – 'getting through' to someone (metaphorically, of course) is a little easier with a power tool!

Gardening tools, compost, pots, seeds and bulbs can all be turned to good magical use, for example to 'grow' wishes. The garden or windowbox are also useful for burying items, which is sometimes recommended. There is no reason why you cannot combine kitchen, garden, office and household tools.

Provided that you abide by the principles of sympathetic magic while letting your imagination take flight, your home and locality can be the source of all the magical ingredients you need!

# blessing for a couple

This should be cast on a waxing Moon, as you are wishing that the couple may prosper. Friday, the day of Venus, which favours lovers, would be ideal.

The use of berries in magic is an ancient tradition stretching back in recorded history as far as the Druids' reverence for mistletoe. Whereas the Druids would harvest the berries from an oak tree with a golden sickle six days after new moon, this spell uses berries that are readily available in most supermarkets or health food shops. Happily, this rules out both the climbing of trees and the wearing of impractical robes.

The purpose of this spell is to construct a magical ring of berries as a charm for a couple starting out on their life together. The berries and fruits used in this spell variously represent sweetness, protection and good health. These are all suitable sentiments to make this blessing charm a special gift for the couple.

You will need...
1 red candle
1 fine embroidery needle
40-cm length of red sewing thread
Up to 50 dried juniper berries
Up to 40 dried cranberries
Up to 30 sultanas

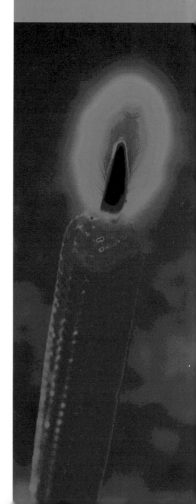

48

# berry spell

You may wish to gather a group of well-wishers to cast this spell, in which case you can pass around the needle and thread and chant together as you each attach a few berries onto the thread.

Light the red candle, saying: **'This candle is lit for two who love well, Hearth fire, bless the hearts who receive this good spell'.**

Thread the needle and tie a large knot in the end of the thread.

Using the needle carefully to pierce them without causing them to split, thread the berries and dried fruits, alternating them to symbolize that you wish the couple good health, protection and sweetness in all parts of their lives together. Repeat the following words, chanting or singing them as you thread: **'Blessed by this spell, All will be well'.**

When you have threaded as many berries and fruits as the length of your thread will allow, fasten it end to end to form a ring.

**Aftercare** Wrap the berry ring carefully and present it to the happy couple. They should hang it above a fireplace or hearth, or in a place they consider to be the heart of the home. It should remain there for as long as the berries stay on the thread, or until they move house, when they should take it with them.

# for getting rid of an unwanted lover's attentions

To be carried out on a waning or dark (new) Moon, as you are working for decrease. It is best cast on Saturday, ruled by Saturn, the planet of restrictions.

Emotional attachment between loved ones is a fine thing, but it can be painful to both parties if it hangs around too long after a relationship has run its course. The natural process of grieving when a romance has ended needs a degree of acceptance, and sometimes this can be a long time coming.

This spell is primarily intended for use in situations where an ex-lover is continuing to pay you unwarranted attention after your relationship has finished. It is designed both to rid you of the attentions and your ex-lover of the attachment that is preventing him/her from recovering and moving on. But the spell is pretty versatile: if your emotions are still a little too attached when a relationship has ended, you can adjust it to help yourself to let go.

**You will need...**
1 wineglass of spring or
   tap water
1 ice-cube tray
1 pan, if using a stove,
   or 1 bowl, if using a
   microwave
1 potted, flowering plant

# ice-cube spell

The first part of this spell takes several hours as it involves making ice-cubes. It would be a good idea to begin this spell in the morning, before everyone else is up, and to return to it in the evening when the ice-cubes are ready. For both parts of the spell, you will need to work in the kitchen.

Hold the glass of water up in both hands and say: **'This is the love that was, This is the attachment** [name of ex-lover] **still feels'.**

Pour the water into the ice-cube tray saying: **'In doing this, I freeze your love and hold it still'.**

Place the ice-cube tray in your freezer or ice-box and leave until completely frozen.

Have a pan or bowl ready, tap out the ice-cubes into it, and place the pan over a low heat on the stove, or put the bowl on the defrost setting in your microwave.

Watching as the ice-cubes melt, say: **'And so shall your attachment dissolve'.**

Pour the water from the ice-cubes into the soil of the potted plant and place the plant outside the house immediately.

**Aftercare** You should not bring the potted plant into the house again, but ensure that you give it to a school sale, charity shop or local hospital as soon as possible after the spell. In this way, you are replacing the banished behaviour and emotions with 'growth' and directing your ex's emotions elsewhere.

# to help you love and value yourself

Carry out this enchantment on a waxing moon as you are working for increase. You want the help of Venus, the love-planet, so Friday is the best day to cast this spell.

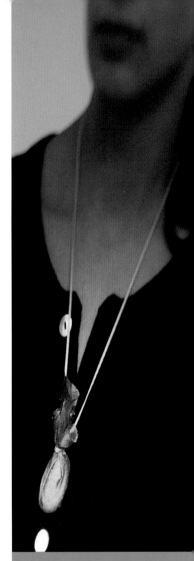

One of the most valuable lessons we ever learn about love is that the less we rely on the regard of others for our self-esteem, the stronger and more 'lovable' we actually become. The purpose of this spell is to help you learn to love and value who you are. It can be repeated many times and used as a tool for confidence building and positive affirmation.

This spell is aimed inwards: it works on you by initiating changes from within. As with all magic, though, its effects will radiate outwards to have an effect on the way other people see or feel about you.

A rose quartz crystal is used here, as both the colour and properties of the stone are associated with the heart and affection. Crystals and stones are now widely available in gift shops and rose quartz is one of the most common.

**You will need...**
1 candle, white or pink
1 small piece of tumbled or polished rose quartz, approximately 3 cm in circumference
5- x 5-cm piece of cloth, any colour but black
60-cm length thin ribbon or cord, any colour

# rose quartz spell

In preparation for this spell, you need to think of all the things you like about yourself – if this is difficult and you are stuck, think about things you admire and like in others and decide which of these attributes you have.

Light the candle.

When you are ready, take your rose quartz stone in your right hand and cover it with your left, saying: **'My name is** [name]**, I am** [name one or more attributes, such as kind, generous, supportive, polite]**'.**

Repeat these two lines naming one attribute each time, until you cannot think of any more.

Place the rose quartz in the centre of the cloth square and say: **'This is the love I bear myself, These are the reasons I value myself'.**

Take the corners of the cloth and tie the stone inside it with the ribbon (or cord), leaving enough ribbon to make it into a necklace.

Hold up the tied pouch by the cord and repeat nine times: **'I am worthy to love, I am worthy of love'.** Place the necklace around your neck so that the stone in the pouch rests over your heart.

**Aftercare** Wear the pouch around your neck for as long as you like or hang it on or over your bed. You can reuse the same stone, cloth and cord every time you feel the need to repeat this spell.

# ③ health

The spells in this chapter offer advice on using magic for good health and healing, a topic that has concerned humans for millennia. They cover a wide range of issues, which include coping with times of ill-health and emotional pain, encouraging general well-being, dealing with fertility issues and diminishing stress.

In matters of emotional distress, particularly, the act of casting a spell can be extremely therapeutic. Stress is a prolific disease in the high-tech 21st century, and many modern lifestyles cultivate stress levels that are capable of causing serious physical and psychological illness. Enabling someone to actively identify and symbolically acknowledge the cause and focus of that suffering can be the first step towards recovery, or finding the courage to ask for help. While spellcraft shouldn't be used to replace the efforts of qualified healers, it helps us to focus upon our personal well-being, which is an issue we would all do well to pay more attention to – and as such, it enhances more conventional forms of medicine.

# for healing

You are working here to decrease suffering, so this spell should be carried out on a waning or dark (new) Moon. Saturday, day of the restrictive planet Saturn, is ideal, but as ever, this spell can be carried out according to need.

There is a long and honourable tradition linking magic with healing through the ages and the spell offered here is a modern-day variation of that ancient wisdom. Spells for healing inevitably involve symbolizing the person or the illness and either diminishing pain and disease or strengthening the healing process.

In the past, the diminishing or taking away of disease or pain has involved removing the illness from the patient and symbolically passing it on to an animal. In this spell, it is passed on without inflicting harm elsewhere.

Bear in mind that 'magic' does not equal 'miracle'. If you or your family member or friend is very sick, then it is the job of qualified healers to give treatment. Spells can send the sick strength, peace and relief, but you cannot halt nature in its tracks: magic works with the natural flow, not against it.

**You will need...**
1 saltshaker, with salt
1 candle, preferably black or brown
1 cotton wool ball or patch approximately 3–4 cm in diameter
A few drops of water to soak cotton wool
1 spare cup
1 radiator, fireplace or sunny windowsill

# cotton wool and salt spell

Place your ingredients at the centre of the room in which you are going to be working and, moving clockwise around the room, shake a circle of salt onto the floor, leaving enough space for you to work in.

Light the candle, saying: **'Saturn, planet of restrictions, Witness and bless this healing spell'.**

Place the cotton wool in the water and, as it soaks up the water, repeat out loud the following words three times: **'Soak up** [name of person's] **pain and take it away'.**

Squeeze as much water as you can out of the cotton wool and into the spare cup. Place both the cotton wool and the cup with the squeezed-out water on a radiator, over a fireplace or on a sunny windowsill and leave undisturbed until the water has evaporated.

**Aftercare** The cotton wool can be thrown away and the cup washed out before returning to its everyday use. Vacuum or sweep up the salt circle as soon as the spell is cast. You can repeat the process as often as needed.

# to reduce grief, anger or guilt

To be cast on a waning or dark (new) Moon for decrease. You can choose any day, but consult the Table of Correspondences (see pages 18–19), to match it to your replacement emotion. For example, if you are replacing 'guilt' with 'positive action', Tuesday, the day of courageous and active Mars, is ideal.

**You will need...**
1 black candle
60-cm length of cord or string
1 kitchen knife, very sharp
2 glass tumblers

Grief at the death of someone close to you is natural. When this gets 'stuck' and halts recovery, however, it can begin to cause emotional damage and affect people around you. Similarly, anger, while a natural and even positive emotion in some situations, can be harmful when it remains unresolved and begins to turn inwards. Guilt, whether justified or not, is another emotion that can live on too long and do damage. This spell is designed to provide release for these types of feelings and can have a very positive psychological effect, especially when the person suffering participates in casting it.

In this spell, the negative emotion is named, then symbolically cut away. You will need to replace what is banished, so carefully think this through if the spell is for yourself, or discuss it with the person you are working for (or with), as appropriate.

# black candle and cord spell

Light the black candle saying: '**I ask the waning moon to take away my** [grief/anger/guilt] **as I no longer want it**'.

Tie a knot in one end of the cord or string to represent your pent-up emotions and another at the other end to represent the replacement.

Take up the cord in your left hand, holding the first knot you tied saying: '**I name you** [grief/anger/guilt]', and then take the second knot in your right hand saying: '**I name you** [replacement]'.

Release your hold, take the knife and cut the cord in the centre.

Place the left-hand cord in a tumbler to your left and the right-hand cord in a tumbler to your right, and say: '**I bury pain and welcome** [replacement]'.

**Aftercare** Untie the knot in the tumbler to your left, and bury the cord deep in your garden where it cannot be disturbed. The other knotted cord should be kept in a safe place until you are confident that the spell has taken effect, and then burned with the knot still intact. Both tumblers should be washed out before returning to normal use.

# for good health

This spell should ideally be cast on a waxing Moon as you are attracting good health. Sunday, or day of the Sun, which is the symbol of well-being, is best.

**You will need...**
1 thumbnail-sized piece of dry bread
1 thimble of red wine
3–4 pinches of salt
1 whole clove
5 x 5-cm piece of red cloth
1 whole nutmeg or a pinch of ground nutmeg
1 gold-coloured coin or coin covered in gold foil
60-cm length of ribbon or cord

This spell is particularly useful for those times when you are beginning to feel run-down and prone to minor illnesses. Casting a spell will never take the place of generally caring for your health, but it will at least give you the edge by working on your own sense of well-being. If common sense is telling you that it is time to see a qualified healer, please do so, as well as casting this spell.

Traditionally, a talisman is a charm in the shape of a pendant or pouch of ingredients, which is designed to promote good energies. Whereas in medieval times the pouches contained everything from arrowheads to animal dung, this talisman is made with everyday ingredients that smell sweeter.

# talisman charm

Prior to casting the spell, you should prepare the bread by soaking it for a few seconds in the wine, then squeezing it out and placing it to dry thoroughly on a sunny windowsill or over a radiator.

Visualize a golden circle all around your working space.

Throw down the salt onto the floor in front of you and step onto it, saying: **'Earth below me, Sun above me, Bless the spell for health I cast before you'**.

Taking the clove, hold it up and say: **'A clove to keep pain at bay'** and then place the clove in the centre of the red cloth.

Take the nutmeg, whether whole or ground, hold it up and say, **'Nutmeg for wholeness'**. Place it with the clove.

Take the now dried, wine-soaked bread, hold it up and say: **'Bread for the earth my body comes from and wine for the water it is born of'**. Place with the other ingredients.

Fasten the ingredients together in the cloth using the ribbon so that it forms a pendant pouch.

**Aftercare** If it is not convenient to wear the talisman all the time, just try to wear it as often as possible and hang it on or over your bed the rest of the time. Keep the contents dry, and this talisman should serve you for a long time. When you feel the need to make a fresh one, dispose of the old one by casting the contents into running water.

# for fertility

Must be cast on a waxing Moon – the symbol of pregnancy and fertility – and on a Monday, day of the Moon, ruler of women's reproductive cycles. There needs to be a clear night sky, with the Moon already risen.

Sometimes, even when the experts have checked everything out and have confirmed that there are no medical problems, people continue to have problems conceiving. If there are no apparent medical reasons why a person or couple should not conceive, then this spell is ideal.

In the past, couples trying for a baby have been advised to make love near or on ancient sacred sites – sometimes with impressive results! This spell does not require any midnight outings to windy hillsides – instead you can get the ingredients for it in your local supermarket. The principles by which this spell operates echo those of the ancients in that, just like the monuments they created, it uses external symbols of fertility and links human reproductive cycles with the cycles of the Earth and Moon.

**You will need...**
- 1 packet mustard and cress seeds, or 1 carton of mustard and cress plants
- 1 white or silver candle
- 1 wineglass of water
- 1 saucer or shallow plate
- 1 square of absorbent cotton, at least 6 x 6 cm

# mustard and cress spell

If the seeds are not readily available in packets, you should harvest them in advance from a carton of mustard and cress as sold in supermarkets or grocers. The wineglass of water should be left out under the light of the Moon for an hour before it is brought in to use in the spell.

Light the candle, saying: **'Grandmother Moon, ruler of the tides and the cycles of new life, Make our fertile tides meet and the seed be planted for new life'.**

Pour the water from the wineglass into the saucer, imagining moonlight pouring into the saucer with it.

Place the absorbent cotton in the saucer and allow it to soak up the water.

Sprinkle the mustard and cress seeds onto the cotton, and as you do, say or chant over and over again: **'She changes everything she touches, And everything she touches changes'.**

Energize this spell by holding the saucer in both hands and repeating the chant at least ten times in total.

Breathe one long warm breath over the seeds and place them on a warm windowsill in the moonlight, or somewhere warm and exposed to daylight.

**Aftercare** The mustard and cress should be kept watered, and, as it grows, allowed to re-seed. You should cut some of the sprouts away and eat them as often as you can. Bless you!

# to promote emotional well-being

This spell is to be cast on a waxing Moon, but not on a full Moon, when feelings generally run high. The best day is Monday, ruled by the Moon, which is associated with the emotions.

It is now generally accepted that our emotional state can adversely influence our physical well-being. Long periods of anxiety, stress or unhappiness can manifest in new or intensified physical illnesses. Happily, the reverse is also true. Although relaxation, calm and a positive attitude cannot conquer or fend off all physical ailments, there is no doubt that they can keep some nasties at bay and give us more of a fighting chance should serious illness come along.

This spell is designed to promote emotional well-being and self-care by balancing out those aspects in your life that cause you grief and joy. The sugar or honey represents the sweetness that such harmony brings. It should accompany a positive decision to change your attitudes, priorities or lifestyle for the sake of emotional balance. Needless to say, where someone has serious emotional problems, they should be encouraged to see a good counsellor.

**You will need...**
- 1 blue candle
- 1 tea bag
- 1 kettle of cold water
- 1 teacup – preferably your favourite (or that of the person for whom you are casting the spell)
- A little milk
- 1 cube or spoonful of sugar, honey or sweetener

# teacup spell

Adapt any of the ingredients to suit your dietary restrictions, if appropriate. If you are doing this spell for someone else, make sure they are nearby to drink the brew when the spell is cast.

Light the candle, saying: **'Element of Water be a witness to this spell, Let my emotions find their balance, Let me find all things are well'.**

Take the tea bag and hold it before the candle, saying: **'In this bag are the pieces of my life that cause me grief and give me joy'.** Place the tea bag to one side.

Set the kettle to boil, and holding the tea bag before the candle, chant the words: **'All will be well'** until the water boils. Place the tea bag in the teacup and pour on the boiling water, removing the bag once the tea is brewed.

Hold the milk before the candle saying: **'Here is nourishment for the spirits'.** Pour into the tea. Hold the sugar, honey or sweetener before the candle saying: **'Here is sweetness that balance brings'.** Stir into the tea.

**Aftercare** Drink the tea right down to the bottom of the cup or give it to the person at whom the spell is aimed. Blow out the candle and save it to light when you are having low moments or are feeling overwhelmed by your emotional responses to life.

# to reduce stress

Cast this spell on a waning Moon as you are banishing, or reducing. Monday is best, as this is the day ruled by the Moon, which is associated with emotional and psychological issues.

Anybody considering the use of magic to reduce stress is probably already more than aware of the damage that unremitting stress can do. Apart from its physical manifestation in illness, it can inhibit the ability to communicate, make decisions, and perform well at work or school, and it can also impact on personal relationships. Too much stress is not only bad for your health, it is bad for your whole life!

This spell is about naming and banishing stress, and downscaling its causes as well as its effects. The planning of this spell, therefore, is a useful exercise in identifying the sources of stress in your life so that you can act to reduce them. Banishing these stresses is generally psychologically beneficial. The magic, of course, is an added bonus.

**You will need...**

1 sewing needle

Up to 5 tea lights to begin with, each one to represent a major source of stress in your life

1 mirror, large enough when flat to support the tea lights

1 saltshaker, filled with salt

# tea light spell

It may be useful to do this in your bedroom. Since you are likely to take your troubles to bed with you, it is appropriate to banish them in the place where you wake up worrying in the early hours!

Before you begin, make a short list of the biggest sources of anxiety in your life. Then, visualize a circle of pale blue light completely surrounding your room.

Take the needle and inscribe one candle at a time with a word or symbol representing a cause of stress, chanting all the while: **'I drop this luggage from my shoulders, I let this anxiety fall from my heart'.** When you have inscribed all of the candles with a different source of stress, place them on the upturned mirror.

Pour an unbroken line of salt in a circle around all the tea lights, saying: **'By this circle they are bound, by this burning they are banished',** until the circle is completed. Still chanting, light the candles one by one and let them burn completely down.

**Aftercare** Allow the tea lights to burn down in a safe place and under supervision, ideally in your bedroom. While they do, why not settle down with a good book, paint your toenails or indulge in a home-facial? This underlines your determination to take care of yourself and do things for you in the future!

# ④ home

Home is our sanctuary from the outside world, somewhere we can be ourselves without judgement or unkindness from others. This chapter gives guidance on making it the safe and nurturing space it should be, whether it is temporary, permanent, a room in a house, an apartment in a block of flats or a room on university campus.

Protecting private space is a perennial human concern, and has played a huge part in magic throughout the years, working to keep away thieves and intruders, as well as just unwelcome callers. And, while there is no magical remedy for unscrupulous landlords or contractors, there are ways you can use spellcraft to supplement the law when it comes to home repairs.

Other sources of annoyance in the home may also be remedied with the use of magic. For example, mislaid property or the trials and tribulations of moving home. If, however, you feel that it is actually the atmosphere of your home that is making you stressed, you may consider having a complete spiritual clean out to leave your intimate space feeling clean, fresh and comfortable.

# to protect your home against theft and intruders

Ideally, this spell should be carried out on a dark (new) Moon for protection. Thursdays are the best choice, as they are ruled by Jupiter, which presides over property matters.

This is based on a very old amulet spell to ward off intrusive strangers from your property. Luckily, the original ingredients are still easily available today in grocery or health food shops. Juniper berries have been a versatile ingredient of spells and charms for centuries, and they make a cheap incense for protection. Today, essence of juniper is used in aromatherapy, herbalism and natural cosmetics to treat a range of conditions, from stomach complaints to oily complexions.

Here, the protective properties of juniper berries are invoked to protect your home by making them into an amulet to hang near the most vulnerable parts of your home – the windows and doors. Sewing berries is a tricky business, so it might be a good idea to practise before casting the spell.

**You will need...**
1 fine, sharp sewing needle
1 tea light
60-cm length of black
    thread for each amulet
Optional – a drop of your
    own blood
40–50 berries for each
    amulet

# juniper berry spell

**21** If you wish to contribute the optional ingredient, ensure that the needle is sterile and that you clean your thumb or finger with antiseptic first. The idea behind putting blood on the thread is so that it will be covered by the protective juniper berries – thus symbolizing your personal safety.

Using the needle, inscribe the tea light with the symbol of Jupiter (see above). Light the candle, saying: **'Generous Jupiter, largest of planets, Witness the spell I cast to protect my home'.**

Thread the needle, doubling the thread and knotting it firmly at the end. If you wish to, prick your thumb or finger with a sterile needle and rub your blood onto the black thread.

Proceed to thread the juniper berries onto the cotton, chanting or singing as you do, **'Banish the bad, Bring in the good',** until you have a string of berries approximately 20 cm long.

Fasten the ends of the thread together, making a circle of berries.

If you are making more than one amulet for your home, repeat the process until you have a sufficient number of berry circles.

**Aftercare** Allow the tea light to burn itself out in a safe place. Position your amulet(s) next to the back door, the front door or the windows – wherever you feel that intruders could get in. When the berries begin to drop off, you can bury them and make new amulets.

# to banish a bad atmosphere

As you are banishing bad vibes, this ritual is most effective when carried out on a waning or dark (new) Moon. Saturday, ruled by the disciplinarian Saturn, is best.

A bad atmosphere in your home can often hang about for years, like a bad smell that nobody can quite pin down. Uneasy vibes can be the result of arguments, unhappy events or, if sensed in a new home, situations you will never know about. Nonetheless, if the atmosphere is bad enough to be noticeable, it's bad enough to warrant a magical spring-clean, which is exactly what this spell does!

Onions – which emit a powerful scent all their own – are used in this spell because of their absorbent properties. Here we use the onions to draw in the bad vibes that make your living space unpleasant, and in disposing of them, get rid of the unwanted atmosphere.

# onion spell

This spell takes place over a twenty-four-hour period, during which you will have to ensure that the pieces of onion you are placing around your home remain undisturbed. The hardest part is having to clean your home prior to casting the spell. The easiest bit is the party you throw afterwards to replace the bad atmosphere with a good one!

Light the black candle saying: **'Saturn, witness this banishing waning/dark Moon, Diminish all bad influences in this** [room]'. Place the candle at the centre of your home.

Peel and cut each onion into quarters, keeping parts of the same onion together as you are going to use one onion for each room. In every room you are cleansing, place a quarter of the onion at each corner, saying: **'Draw in the bad atmosphere of this room completely'.**

Let the candle burn itself out and leave the onion pieces overnight.

Twenty-four hours later, gather in the onion quarters and remove them from the premises immediately, even if this is just to leave them outside your door until you get a chance to bury them.

Light the white candle and place it at the centre of your home. Holding the bowl of water in your left hand and the salt in your right, say: **'Purity of salt, I add you to cleansing water to bless my home'.** Sprinkle the salted water in a clockwise circle around each room, saying: **'Bless and cleanse this living space',** until you have done this in each room.

**Aftercare** The onions should be buried in earth a good distance away from your home. Throw a party to celebrate the shiny new atmosphere in your home and to replace the negative old one with something nice!

# for moving into a new home

As this spell is predominantly about communications and transit, it is best carried out on Wednesday, presided over by Mercury, planet of communications and commerce. As you are working for positive action, cast your spell on a waxing moon.

**You will need...**
1 square of yellow or orange fabric, approximately 15 x 15 cm
1 newspaper, open at the property or 'letting' section
1 indelible ink pen
Either staples, a needle and cotton (any colour) or a length of ribbon
35-cm garden or bamboo cane

This spell can be used whether you are wishing to sell, buy or rent a new house, apartment or room. Moving into a new home is an event that is right up there amongst the most stressful life situations. As well as the psychological and physical upheaval involved, there are the worries about money, legal issues, timing and communications. Unless all these four issues operate together, it can cause major stress. This spell is designed to help the transition go as smoothly as possible.

The use of a flag in this spell is based upon three different, yet appropriate principles. Firstly, the flag can be used as a signal to say: 'Get me out of here!' Secondly, the symbols on it act as a declaration of intent. Lastly, the energy raised by the flag flapping in the wind is significant as this spell is to encourage your wish to be carried by the element most associated with communications and transit – Air.

# flag spell

 Ideally, this spell should be carried out in your present home as this is the starting point of your move. It is from here that you will begin the journey to your new home.

Visualize a circle of quicksilver (mercury) flowing all around the space in which you are going to work. Take the square of fabric in both hands and visualize the desired outcome of your efforts to move home.

When you have fixed this vision firmly in your mind, chant the following until you feel thoroughly energized: '**Now quicksilver, quickly flow, To my new home I shall go**'.

Lay the fabric, or flag, flat on the property section of the newspaper and, taking the indelible ink pen, draw the symbol of Mercury (see above) in the centre. To the left-hand side, draw a horizontal arrow pointing to the symbol, and to the right-hand side, write your first name, leaving out all the vowels.

Using either the staples, needle and thread or ribbon, fasten the cloth to the pole firmly and say: '**Mercury make my move swift, Air carry my wishes**'.

**Aftercare** Fly this flag out of a window in your present home, making sure, of course, that it is secure. Leave it where it is until your move is achieved, when you should take it with you to your new home, cut it up and dispose of the remnants in the nearest recycling facility.

# to ward off unwanted visitors

As this spell is to ward people off, it should be carried out on a dark (new) Moon. Saturday, governed by Saturn, the restrictive and forbidding planet, is best for casting this spell.

Even the most sociable person needs some 'down-time' occasionally. You do not have to be a hermit to want your personal space respected. In fact, it is often the more gregarious among us who have to force this issue; our social circles tend to be wider and our sociability means that we are more likely to attract casual 'drop-in' visits. Even though the majority of these calls are friendly and well-intended, everyone needs a break from company and this spell will buy you a little much-needed space.

If you receive constant visits from over-friendly neighbours, friends, relatives or inconsiderate roomies, then it is definitely hag-stone time! Hag-stones are traditionally stones with a hole worn through their middle by the sea. In the past, they were placed on or tied to gateposts to keep trouble at bay. Since natural hag-stones are quite rare, this spell uses a more modern and practical version, which works just as effectively as the genuine article.

**You will need...**
1 sharp embroidery needle
1 tea light
1 black indelible ink pen
3 or more scallops, oysters, clams or other similarly shaped shells, gathered from a seashore or bought in a shop
15 cm strong black thread
1 nail, and a hammer or heavy stone

# hag-stone spell

This spell requires patience and delicacy – and may involve keeping some spare shells to hand if all does not go according to plan on the first try!

Visualize a circle of hands, palms outwards, held up in the same gesture that the police use to halt traffic, all around the space in which you are going to work.

Using the needle, inscribe the shape of a hand held in the same gesture into the wax surface of the tea light. Light the wick, saying: **'Saturn, with this sign I keep away unwanted visitors'.**

With the indelible ink pen, draw the same symbol on each of the shells.

Take the needle and very slowly drill a hole through each shell. Pass the black thread through all three, make a loop and fasten.

Hold the shells up by the thread before the candle and say: **'By my will and with this sign, A quiet space and quiet time, Visitors who welcome be, Can pass through this and come to me, I nail these hag-stones to my mast, That those unwelcome shall not pass'.**

**Aftercare** Allow the tea light to burn down completely in a safe place, and at the first opportunity nail your hag-stones to a doorpost that represents the entrance to your home, be it a gatepost to a house, or the doorframe of your room if you share an apartment.

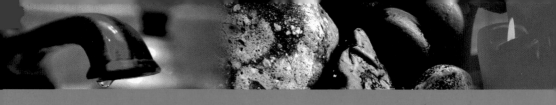

# the magical home

Creating a magical home is a fun, therapeutic and inexpensive experience. It is not just about creating areas in which to cast spells – it is about actively redefining the space at your disposal and making it an enchanted place for you and those you invite into it.

## decorating your world

If you are lucky enough to have a house or an apartment with several rooms, you might consider decorating them in accordance with the five elements. A study, for example, would be ideal as the domain of Air, which oversees matters of thought, communication and knowledge. You could feature the colour yellow and decorate with feathers, maps, charts and other symbols representing the various functions of Air. This magically enhances the space where you do your thinking, work or study. A bathroom, similarly, could be transformed into a place of well-being and balance using symbols of Water, the element of healing and harmony.

If you are limited to one room, you can still make your home space magical in a number of ways. One way is to adapt the elemental theme by dividing it up into areas dedicated to different elements. Another way is to create an 'orientation' feel to the room, using the walls, floor and ceiling to display symbols of the cycle of the day, the year or the phases of the moon. If you decided to represent the day, images of the rising sun could be displayed in the

east of your room, the noonday sun in the south, the setting sun in the west and so on. The phases of the moon could be displayed on the walls around your room. A star map, using fluorescent stick-on stars available in many toy stores, could go on the ceiling, providing an after-dark replica of the night sky. Orientating your room in this way will help you to focus on your magical work and get a sense of your place in the universe – both essential aspects of spellcraft.

## a sacred space

Whether you have a large space to play with, or very little, it is possible to build a little magical shrine in a corner. Space-saving corner shelves are cheap and available from most furniture or DIY shops. Constructing your own magical space is an empowering experience. Such shrines are also easily adapted should you want to change things or shift your life focus. When you are concerned with stability and material matters, build a cairn of pebbles lit by tea lights. When you are concentrating more on your emotional life, put representations of water in your corner. This could be a wineglass full of tinted water, with glass pebbles and mirrors, and maybe even a backdrop of stick-on silver stars.

Having a space, however small, into which you can put images and symbols that are meaningful to you, is very life-affirming and comes highly recommended.

# effecting speedy home repairs

Ideally, as this spell resonates with the mirror image of the half-Moon, it should be carried out at either a waxing or waning half-Moon. For maximum impact, a Monday is best, but the Moon phase should take precedence over the actual day if the two do not coincide.

This spell is great for getting things moving when your living space needs repairs. You can use it whether you are a tenant, relying on a slow-moving or reluctant landlady/landlord, or a home-owner trying to get a contractor to complete work satisfactorily and quickly.

Mirrors are used in magic for a number of purposes, and one of these is to 'reflect' good or bad deeds back upon the person responsible. This spell uses a double mirror theme – it firstly reflects your wishes towards those in control of the repairs, and secondly, ensures that their action (or inaction) is reflected back upon themselves. Bouncing the consequences back to the person responsible is not a curse – it is simply a way of ensuring that those consequences are realized and obligations are met.

## You will need...

- 1 white, silver or blue candle
- 2 mirrors of similar size or a double-sided shaving mirror, one side magnified
- 1 blue or black dry-wipe marker of the type used on whiteboards

# double mirror spell

Spend some time on the chanting part of this spell and take care to recognize the 'shift' in energy, which may be felt in the energy points at the base of the spine, the stomach and the chest.

Visualize a crescent of moonlight halfway around the space in which you are working, and then complete the circle with a grey, dark blue or black crescent.

Light the candle, saying: **'By the moon's light, I cast my will, By its dark shadow, I cast the (in)action of** [name of landlord/contractor]**'.**

Take two mirrors, or a double-sided mirror, and in the first (non-magnified) one, say to your own reflection: **'It is my will that repairs are completed *now*!'** Really emphasize the **'*now!*'**

Hold the second mirror, or magnified side of the double mirror, and draw a vertical line down the centre, saying: **'Here are the options for** [name]**'s response – positive or negative. May the action they choose be reflected back upon them in equal part'.**

Chant the following until you feel the shift of energy, described above, and feel that the spell is fully 'charged': **'As the mighty oceans flow, let it be so, let it be so'.**

**Aftercare** Place the mirror or double mirror in the front window of your home, with 'your' side facing inwards and the other facing out. Leave this in place until the repairs are completed.

# for the return of lost property

Best cast on a waxing Moon, as you are requesting return. The most auspicious day for this spell is Thursday, ruled by Jupiter, which presides over property matters, fortune, generosity and natural justice.

This spell is designed to retrieve missing items. Although its purpose is very specific and simple, the spell is really very versatile and can be used in many situations. You can use it if you have mislaid an article that you would really like to see again, if an object has been removed without your permission or if you have lent something to someone who, in spite of numerous requests, has not returned it.

As with much of sympathetic magic, there is a very literal element to the choice of ingredients here. Two aspects of rubber bands are put to use – they are designed to keep things together and they 'bounce'. This spell aims to return the missing item to its rightful owner by drawing it in, just as a rubber band retracts when stretched, its 'bounciness' ensuring that the object comes bouncing back to you!

**You will need...**
- 1 purple candle, or white candle with the Jupiter symbol carved on its side (see above right)
- 1 large box of at least 150 office-quality rubber bands
- 1 large envelope
- 1 first-class stamp
- 1 pen, any colour ink

# rubber band spell

Cast this spell where there is a hard floor, a wall and space enough to throw a ball against the wall and let it bounce back to you safely.

Light the candle, saying: **'I call upon Jupiter the generous, Jupiter the fortunate, Jupiter the just, to witness this spell for the return of my** [item]'.

Take one rubber band from the box and tie it in knots to form a rough sphere.

Wrap consequent rubber bands around it to form a ball, chanting all the while: **'I call upon my** [item] **wherever it may be, To stretch out like these rubber bands and come right back to me!'**

When the ball is completed and all bands have been used, turn towards the wall and bounce the ball against it, allowing it to hit the ground on its journey back to you. Repeat until this action has been carried out nine times in all, saying on each throw: **'Come back to me!'**

Address the large envelope to yourself. Unravel the rubber bands, place them all in the envelope and seal.

Place the postage stamp firmly on the envelope saying: **'Safe and swift return!'** Blow out the candle.

**Aftercare** Post the envelope as soon after completing the spell as possible. When you receive it, do not open but keep it in a safe place until the missing item is returned.

# ⑤ family, friends and neighbours

This chapter offers a variety of spells that concern, in one way or another, your social, family and neighbourhood groups. These are the circles we move in on a daily basis, and as such, can be taken for granted – at least until something changes or goes wrong. These spells are directed at investing a little time and sweetness in order to keep these important relationships healthy.

Making new friends when you move to a new neighbourhood, school, university or job can be pretty daunting, for example. The spell given here is designed to bring you opportunities to make new friends. Protecting and nurturing children also forms a large part of the family and neighbourhood life and the spells reflect this.

Living in close quarters with other people sometimes engenders quarrelling, whether between family or flatmates. This chapter will provide some enjoyable ways to lift the atmosphere in difficult situations, and suggest ways to work against gossip and disruptive behaviour, offering relief from the misery caused by bad neighbours.

# blessing for a new baby

Make this charm on a waxing Moon, as you are asking for increase and prosperity. Any day, with the possible exception of Saturday, is fine, but consult the Table of Correspondences (see pages 18–19) to select a day in line with the wishes you would like to emphasize.

**You will need...**
1.5-m length of yellow ribbon, approximately 5 mm wide
1 twisted willow hoop, available from florists or gift shops; alternatively, a wire hoop fitted with padding and covered with a decorative fabric. Size approximately 15 cm in diameter.
Variety of colour ribbons (not black), all approximately 40 cm long and 5 mm wide

Magic is a great way to contribute to happy occasions. This spell offers you the opportunity to be a 'Good Fairy' and bless a new baby in a manner worthy of a fairy-tale godparent. It allows you to offer a meaningful and unique welcoming gift to a new small person, whether this is a new baby brother, sister, cousin, niece, nephew, the child of a friend or a new addition of your very own.

This spell enables you to work some magic on the baby's behalf and provide a charm to be hung in the nursery. It is very simple to make, and the ingredients described here can be exchanged and replaced to suit your needs. What really matters is the magic and the good intent that you are putting into this lovely charm.

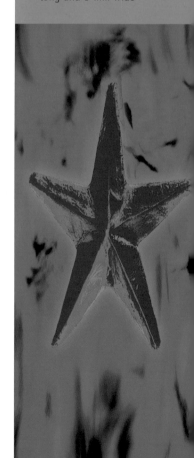

# cradle-charm spell

The wishes listed in this spell are just suggestions and can be replaced with those you feel are more appropriate. You may want to think about these in advance.

Visualize a circle of golden light all around the space in which you are going to work.

Tie the end of the yellow ribbon to the top of the hoop, and loop the ribbon across the hoop to form a five-pointed star.

When you have completed the star, coil the remainder of the yellow ribbon evenly around the hoop and tie it off.

Tie the other ribbons in a bunch onto the bottom of the hoop (the star should point up) and hold it aloft, saying: '[baby's name]; **I wish you good health, I wish you a sufficiency of food, warmth and shelter, I wish you many causes of happiness in your life, I wish you the joy of good companions, May the days be kind to you, And the nights be comfort, I wish you welcome'.**

**Aftercare** The charm is a decoration, not a toy, as ribbons can be dangerous to babies. Hang it safely and securely in the room where the baby sleeps, but keep it well out of reach.

# to prevent quarrels between siblings

As the spell is seeking to improve relationships, it should be cast on a waxing Moon, preferably close to the beginning of its cycle. Friday, the day of Venus, the harmony and friendship planet, is ideal.

**You will need...**
1 candle, gold for peace,
    pink for affection or
    silver for ties that bind
50-cm length of black wool
50-cm length of white wool
50-cm length of red wool
1 sharp pair of scissors

Fighting and squabbling between young brothers and sisters is a natural part of family life. When rivalry persists, however, or when their fights become so persistent that they disrupt the peace of the household, it is time to do something. This type of constant combat can be very wearying whether you are a long-suffering onlooker or an active competitor. Accordingly, this spell is designed to calm things down in a very special way.

The Bracelet spell uses a weaving motif, which in magical terms is a good way of recognizing and respecting differences, rather than denying or erasing them. The act of weaving separate lengths of material together, each representing a different perspective, serves to build a harmonious pattern where individual strands combine forces and become much stronger than when apart. Weaving is a very apt symbol of strength through cooperation and friendship, and so is particularly relevant to quarrelling siblings.

# bracelet spell

The black and white lengths of wool or yarn represent each of the warring sides in the quarrel, and the red represents the blood or other relationship that binds them together. Decide in advance which of the parties is represented by black and which by white.

Visualize a circle of rainbow-coloured light all around the area in which you are working.

Light the candle and say, as appropriate: **'May those who presently war against each other be bound together by** [affection/ peace/the ties of their relationship]'.

Knot the three colours of yarn together, approximately 1 cm from the end, and plait them, chanting: **'Love cannot fail; Peace will prevail'.** When the lengths are completely plaited, tie off in a secure knot.

Cut the plait exactly in half with the scissors, and knot the cut ends so they do not unravel. You will have enough for two bracelets, one each for the quarrelling pair.

**Aftercare** Let the candle burn down safely. Encourage the feuding pair to wear a bracelet each. Tie them onto their wrists yourself if possible, but if not, don't tie them in advance as they will need to fit the wrists of the individuals exactly. The bracelets should be kept until they drop off, and buried when the quarrelling ends or nailed to a wall to remind the former combatants of the bad old days.

# to prevent a child's nightmares

Preferably, this spell should be enacted on a waning or dark (new) Moon as the aim is to banish something. Saturday, day of the disciplinarian and restrictive planet Saturn, is ideal. What is vital is that you perform it just prior to the turning of an incoming tide.

This spell is aimed at preventing bad dreams in young ones, and is especially effective if you can involve the child in question in the construction of the spell itself. Besides being good fun, the building of a sand castle can be a powerful psychological aid to children, especially as they watch the sea wash in and take the 'dream castle' away.

Sand and water are particularly significant to the nature of dreams. Both elements are shifting and transitory and anything we make from sand can be washed away by the tide, rather in the same way as the morning washes away the dreams of the previous night. In fact, in some cultures, dreams are known as 'castles in the air'.

**You will need...**
- 1 sandy beach or tidal shoreline
- 1 child's bucket and spade
- 1 wooden stick, approximately 8 cm long
- 1 black felt-tip or ink pen
- 4 x 5-cm piece of paper – any colour
- 1 stick or tube of paper glue

# sand castle spell

This spell can be carried out with or without the direct involvement of the child in question. Remember to give yourself enough time to construct the castle and complete your chanting before the tide comes in.

Build a large sand castle close to the edge of the water, chanting as you build: **'Bad dreams go away, Don't come back, Just stay away, Leave** [child's name] **free to run and play, Bad dreams go away'**.

When the castle is finished, take the stick and draw a circle in the sand all the way around you and the castle, leaving yourself enough room to sit behind the castle, facing the incoming tide.

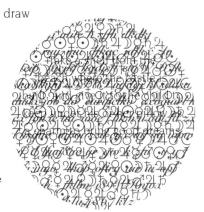

Draw a skull and crossbones on the piece of paper and glue it to the stick.

Stick this flag into the castle, saying: **'The tide take you, The waves break you'**.

Let the incoming tide wash the castle away.

**Aftercare** You should replace the banished nightmares with something appropriate for the little one's bedroom. For example, a herbal pillow from a gift shop to aid sleep or a crystal to hang in the window, so that the child can enjoy seeing rainbows. Alternatively, you could prepare the charm described in the next spell to hang in the bedroom.

# to mend quarrels

This spell works to bring harmony so if you can, cast it on a
waxing Moon. Friday, the day of Venus, the patron of friendship
and harmony, is best.

The unpleasantness generated when family
members or friends quarrel has a tendency to spread
and affect innocent bystanders. Watching those close
to you fall out can be very distressing, and the effort
of staying out of the firing line can be wearing.

Before you consider casting this spell, check that
your own motives are sensible. There is a time to
stand up for yourself and be heard, and a limit to
tolerance, particularly when someone close to you is
behaving badly. Be realistic – simply thinking that
everyone should be nice to each other, regardless of
the situation, may lead you to miss the point.

When a quarrel has become petty, or has dragged
on to the point where everyone has forgotten who
said what and why they were insulted in the first
place, it is perfectly justifiable to want to break the
deadlock. This spell is designed for such a situation.

**You will need...**
2 20-cm lengths of pink
embroidery thread –
each a different shade
1 embroidery needle
6 x 6-cm piece of 16-, 18-
or 20-count Aida or
Harbinger/cross stitch
fabric, available from
craft shops

# cross stitch spell

If you are an accomplished cross stitcher, you may prefer to draw a chart of the initials of the two warring parties entwined and work from that. If you are less experienced, draw two overlapping circles onto the fabric ready to stitch along. Cross stitches are stitched bottom left to top right, then the overlay stitch travels from bottom right to top left. Keep the stitches consistent in tension and direction for a smooth finish.

Visualize a circle of pale green light all around the area in which you are working.

Select a shade of pink for one feuding party and another for their opponents, and thread your needle with the appropriate shade for the first faction.

Following your outline, and starting from the centre, stitch one circle or set of initials to represent the party.

When this is completed, re-thread your needle with the shade you selected for the second camp and stitch the second circle or set of initials to represent them.

Holding the embroidery in both hands, say aloud: **'Stitched together, the split is mended, By my spell the quarrel is ended'.**

**Aftercare** Put the embroidery away in a safe place and when the quarrel is ended, make a replica, frame both and offer them as gifts to both parties. You can elaborate on the original design to enhance its decorative aspect, but be sure to give equal attention to both; after all, you wouldn't wish this to be the cause of another quarrel!

# needlework in spellcraft

The craft of needlework provides a range of tools and techniques that are eminently suitable for use in the craft of magic. There is a symbolic parallel between the two in that both are concerned with mending or creating something of use, or of beauty. The language of both crafts also frequently crosses over. For example, we speak of 'weaving' magic and 'casting' spells. Using the ancient traditions of sympathetic magic, the contents of the needlework box are also ideal for use in modern spells. With a little imagination, the magician may assemble a diverse range of tools by venturing no further than the average haberdashery department.

## a versatile medium

A needle dangled by a thread over the abdomen of a pregnant women has long been used to predict the sex of the baby. If the needle rotates deasil (clockwise), it will be a boy, if it goes widdershins (counter clockwise), it will be a girl.

The application of pins to poppets (or human-shaped dolls) is used to influence or heal. For example, to make feelings of remorse or pity 'pierce' the subject, or to help 'pin down' an illness.

Coloured curtain cords can be used to represent the elements, make spell-knots, witches' ladders and to symbolically 'bind' items. Ribbons, cords and threads can also fasten charms in a pouch. Choose colours from the Table of Correspondences (pages 18–19).

## tailor-made solutions

Using thick thread and Aida or Harbinger cloth, which is suitable for cross stitch, it is possible to cast a spell using embroidered symbols, runes, pictures and writing. The patch of embroidery can then be hung in a special place until the desired changes have come to pass.

Felt, muslin or cotton can be used to make a 'poppet' for healing spells. Cut out a double-thickness in paper-doll shape, stuff with the appropriate dried herbs, or even cotton dabbed with the appropriate essential oil, and sew the edges together.

Safety pins are particularly suitable for protection spells. It is possible to construct a perfectly good travel spell by placing safety pins in the head, hands and feet of a poppet. Alternatively, a small felt square or pin cushion studded all over with fastened safety pins makes a lovely, magical gift for a young person who is leaving home to go to university.

Quarrelling friends can be brought together with a patchwork spell. Using differently coloured or patterned pieces of cloth to represent the parties in question, sew them together and chant your intent – for example: '**I sew the patches end to end and bring together warring friends**', or whatever you feel appropriate to the situation. The contrasting pieces symbolize their differences and the act of sewing brings them together in spite of these.

# for harmony between flatmates

Working to promote harmony is easiest on a waxing Moon. This spell can be carried out on Monday for creating a connection, Wednesday for improving communications, Thursday for friendship and generosity, Friday for harmony and peace or Sunday for general well-being. Do not, however, choose Saturday of stubborn Saturn, or Tuesday, day of war-like Mars!

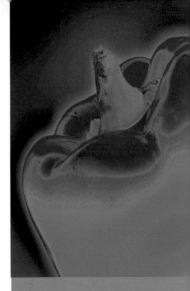

Living with people who fight can be horrible. Your home should be a place to relax without people ruining the atmosphere. The truth is that you cannot make people like each other or prevent them from quarrelling. You can, however, do something to promote a harmonious atmosphere that will not only provide support for you in your living space, but may well calm down your battling buddies and reduce arguments to a minimum.

This spell works partly on the principle of getting the enemies to sit down and eat together; occasional communal meals are good psychological groundwork in any case. It is also based on reversing the symbol of 'stirring', which has come to mean 'causing trouble'. Here, the symbol is used to combine and mix together the attributes of the two fiery ones in a latter-day cauldron (a wok!) to make a magical meal.

## You will need...
1 tbsp cooking oil
1 large wok
1 tsp ginger root, freshly chopped
5 cloves garlic, chopped
100 g broccoli, chopped and sliced
1 red pepper/pimento, sliced
1 yellow pepper/pimento, sliced
100 g each beansprouts, carrots, mushrooms (any type), chopped/sliced finely
1 steaming kettle full of boiling water
200 g tofu, chopped into cubes
2 tbsp soy sauce
1 tbsp vinegar
1 tsp honey

# stir-fry spell

Heat the oil in the wok and add the ginger and garlic. Stir until the mixture is simmering.

Stir in the broccoli, peppers, bean sprouts, carrots and mushrooms, adding boiling water as necessary, until vegetables are heated, but still fresh and crisp.

Add the tofu and the soy sauce.

As you stir in the vinegar, say: **'I cannot stop you being sour',** and adding the honey say: **'But sweetness comes home from this hour'.**

Serve onto plates straight away and enjoy with your flatmates. Ensure throughout the meal that you steer the conversation away from any contentious issues.

**Aftercare** Wash the plates and pans yourself on this occasion; you don't want quarrels emerging as a result of your meal. Encourage one of your flatmates to make a spicy chilli or curry for the next communal meal – they may as well cook fiery if they are going to be fiery and at least you reap the benefits! Enjoy the improved atmosphere in your home.

# to find new friends

This spell is best cast on a waxing Moon, as you are attracting people to you. Friday, day of Venus, the planet that rules over different types of love, including friendship, is the best day on which to enact it.

At various times in our lives we may encounter situations that require us to move in a new direction socially. These changes often involve having to meet new people and build new relationships. Whether you are moving to a new school or college, changing jobs, or moving home – or simply wish to change or widen your circle of friends and acquaintances, this spell is for bringing new friends into your life.

This is an especially nice way of sending out the right magical signals that you are ready for new companions. Since it is good company that makes the journey of life sweeter, this spell uses sugar both as a symbol of the friendship you have to offer, and as an attraction to the sweet natures of other like-minded individuals.

**You will need...**
6 sugar cubes, white or brown
1 hot drink, for when the spell is cast

# sugar cube spell

Cast this spell in the open, preferably under a starry night sky or at dusk when the first star appears. You can remove yourself to a quiet hillside, or carry this out in your back garden – as long as you are in the open. If you do not eat sugar, the sixth sugar cube should be replaced by an alternative sweetener.

Hold the sugar cubes in your cupped hands, fix your sight on the brightest star you can see, raise them up and say: **'Starlight, Starbright, Brightest star that I can see, Bring bright new friendships, Here to me'.**

Crumble five of the sugar cubes, and holding the last sugar cube in your left hand, cast the crumbled sugar towards the star you have fixed your sight on with your right hand.

Bow to your star and go back indoors carrying the last sugar cube.

**Aftercare** Once indoors, make a hot drink for yourself and dissolve the sugar in it. Drink it right down to the last drop. New friends should come into your life within one Moon cycle. When they do appear, remember to light a votive candle for Venus, the evening star, the next time you see her in the sky. This spell can be repeated as often as you wish, but do remember that when sweetness comes into your life, you should also give it in return.

# to stop gossip

This is a binding spell, and needs to take place either when the Moon is waning (last quarter), or on a dark (or new) Moon. The planetary correspondence for restrictions is Saturn, so the spell is best carried out on a Saturday.

**You will need...**
1 black candle
1 dandelion clock, with seeds
20 x 20 cm piece of cloth
2 30-cm lengths black thread
1 yellow dandelion flower
1 white candle

The type of gossip against which this spell is directed refers to harmful untruths put about by thoughtless or vicious tongues, either male or female. Whether it is neighbourhood talk or misinformation being spread among friends and acquaintances, being the subject of unpleasant gossip can be distressing.

Gossip may have one identifiable origin or it may have spread so far that it is difficult to tell where the information is coming from, or even why it started. Either way, the life cycle of the dandelion provides an excellent symbol of this process – once the seeds are borne on the wind, they spread far and wide, growing into plants, which in time bear more seeds and so the process of spreading continues. When dandelions penetrate a patch of soil, they take over, stealing essential nutrients from other plants and spread like wildfire. Unpleasant gossip can have much the same effect by dominating our attention, taking over from what is good in our lives and removing the emotional nourishment we all need to stay healthy.

# dandelion spell

Visualize a circle of white light around the space in which you are going to work. Light the black candle. Holding the dandelion clock, name it as the person spreading the rumours: '**I name you** [gossip's] **lies**'.

Without disturbing the seeds, cover the entire head with the cloth, gathering the ends at the stalk, or just beneath. Using one of the black threads, firmly tie the ends of the cloth, saying: '**By my right and by my will, I hold the source of gossip still, May all your seeds, as all your deeds, Blow in your own garden free, And flourish there for all to see**'. Now hold the yellow flower and name it as the tongue of the person spreading rumours: '**I name you** [gossip's] **wicked tongue**'.

Wind the other length of black thread around the flower's base, drawing the petals together and closing the flower tightly. Fasten the thread firmly and say: '**As I bind these petals, So I bind your tongue from speaking harm**'.

Place both dandelions before the black candle, saying: '**Saturn aid me as I cast this charm, Bind and restrict** [him/her/them] **from speaking all harm. So mote it be**'. Light the white candle, saying: '**May the light of truth bless those who presently speak harm**'. Blow out the black candle.

**Aftercare** Allow the white candle to burn out safely. Keep the dandelions in a safe place until the spell has done its work; then burn them. If it is practical, invite the gossip(s) for a salad made from the washed leaves of a dandelion grown from one of the seeds. In this way, the gossip(s) will literally eat his/her words and draw nourishment from doing so.

# to bind disruptive neighbours

As this is a binding spell, it should be performed on a waning or dark (new) Moon. Saturday, the day of the restrictive planet Saturn, is ideal.

In today's overcrowded world, it is not uncommon for people to disturb the neighbourhood. If you are affected by the behaviour of your neighbours – whether they keep you awake at night with loud music or arguments, or they show a lack of respect for your privacy or property – this spell will help to restore the peace and will enable you to relax once more in your home.

Before casting this spell, it is important that you sit down and think carefully about how bad the behaviour of your neighbours really is. Are they genuinely inconsiderate or are your own expectations unreasonable? For that matter, are you always a good neighbour yourself? If you are satisfied that they really are in the wrong, you should try talking to them calmly and reasonably, stressing that you are keen to maintain a good relationship with them. If this doesn't work, then it is time for a little magic.

**You will need...**
- 1 black candle
- 3 pipe cleaners for each bad neighbour
- 1 nail for each bad neighbour
- 1 clean, empty preserve or pickle jar, with lid

# pipe cleaner and nail spell

Identify a spot of secluded earth that won't be disturbed. If you live in an apartment far from green spaces, you can use a flowerpot and potting compost; prepare them before you start.

Visualize a dark circle all around the place where you are working.

Light the candle saying: **'Saturn, ruler of restriction, Lend your energy to the casting of this spell to bind the bad behaviour of** [name of neighbour]'.

Twist one pipe cleaner into the shape of two legs and a trunk. Link another to it to form two arms, and twist on a third, looped in the shape of a head. If you are making more than one, wait until you have done all of them before proceeding.

Take each pipe cleaner person individually and say: **'I name thee** [name of neighbour] **and Bad Neighbour. I restrict your actions so'.** On the last word, twist the trunk of the body around the nail so that it appears to be going through the body.

Place the figure in the jar straight away. Repeat the above for each figure as appropriate.

When they are all in the jar, seal the lid. Bury it immediately in your chosen area of earth.

**Aftercare** You should ensure that the jar remains undisturbed for the duration of your neighbours' residence.

# ⑥ prosperity

It is perfectly all right to send out requests via the magical 'web' to enable you to attain something that you need. The spells in this chapter should, however, be based on reasonable expectation. Over and above that, and your demands will be straining against the magical network. Connection is the domain of Spirit, element of transformation. Balance and equity are integral characteristics of Spirit, and its symbol, the web, signals our interconnection with all of existence – so put any thoughts about the accumulation of huge amounts of money from your mind!

Many of the spells in this chapter draw upon the Earth theme, using planting and growing as a technique of ensuring a sufficiency of money or to gain a particular item. Spells can also be effective for exploring breaks from the workaday world, setting up a new enterprise and borrowing money.

The last spell is to encourage your own personal wheel of fortune to turn, and involves making good-luck charms – and eating sweets! May the spells in this chapter bring you good fortune and sweetness both.

# for enough money

Working to attract increase requires a waxing Moon, which is close to full. Ideally, this spell should be cast on Monday, day of the Moon, which resembles a silver coin when it is full.

There is an old saying that 'money doesn't grow on trees'. The inspiration for this spell comes from the sentiment that we can't always have what we want, which is why the spell aims to supply enough rather than an excess of money. Sufficiency here implies need rather than want, and refers to the basic requirements of food, shelter, warmth, bills and enough money to ward off misery.

The 'money tree' referred to here is a succulent plant with round, coin-shaped leaves – its Latin name is *Crassula ovata*. If this exact plant is not available in your vicinity, you should use a plant that has round leaves, if at all possible.

There is a very long tradition of making offerings to trees in magic. The plant in this spell works as a symbol representing your financial situation. Drawing upon the principles of sympathetic magic, by giving it food, drink and a coin to represent wealth, you are also encouraging the health of your finances.

## You will need...
- 1 green candle, or a white candle inscribed with the sign for Earth (see above right)
- 1 'money tree' or equivalent plant
- 15 g salt
- 1 trowel or dessert spoon
- 1 small piece of bread, rolled into a ball
- A few drops of red wine
- 1 silver-coloured coin of any denomination

# money tree spell

 Locate a spot in your house where the money tree can grow safely and undisturbed. You will need to perform the spell in the same room and keep the plant in this spot thereafter.

Visualize a circle of pale moonlight all around the place in which you are working.

Light the candle saying: **'Element of Earth, Disc of the Moon, Grant me sufficiency, May my fortunes grow and prosper with my money tree'**.

Place the money tree in the spot where it will remain and take one step backwards.

Throw the salt on the ground in front of you and step forwards onto it saying: **'My wishes are grounded and rooted in earth'**.

With the trowel or spoon, make a tunnel in the soil under the plant.

Dip the bread in the wine, and place it in the tunnel along with the coin. Rearrange soil around plant.

**Aftercare** Vacuum or sweep up the salt after the spell is cast. Tend your money tree very carefully, and either follow the instructions that come with the plant or get advice from your local garden centre or library.

# for the success of a new enterprise

Since you are attracting success you should work with a waxing Moon. This spell is best carried out on Wednesday, ruled by Mercury, the communications and commerce planet.

This spell is designed to get a new enterprise off to a really good start. Whether you are planning to sell home-baked biscuits on your break, run a mail-order company over the internet or set up a volunteer bureau, this will get things moving.

It uses an up-to-date version of an ancient principle: the use of imagery in sympathetic magic. The invention of photography has been very useful to the evolution of practical magic, as we are now able to use more exact likenesses of people or items. Photographs have the added dimension of being personal (an important part of sympathetic magic), of being an imprint of a person or thing actually present at the time the image was 'made'.

For this spell, you will need a photograph of something directly related to the enterprise you are setting up, such as a logo, van or someone involved in your venture.

**You will need...**
- 1 yellow candle, or white candle inscribed with the symbol of Mercury (see above right)
- 1 photograph of the appropriate person or item directly related to the enterprise
- 1 envelope, large enough for the photograph
- 1 pen, any colour

# photograph spell

Ideally, this spell should be carried out in the place where you are planning to base your activities. If for any reason this is not possible, however, any private space will suffice.

Light the candle and visualize its light filling the space in which you will be working towards your new enterprise.

Hold the photograph in both hands, concentrate on the image and visualize clients or interested parties contacting you to participate in or use the services offered.

Still focusing on the image, say: **'I call upon Mercury, I call upon Air to boost my** [business/enterprise/scheme] **and reflect my hard work in success. May I build upon a good beginning'.**

Place the photograph in the envelope and seal it.

Take the pen and write on the front of the envelope in large, block-capital letters: SUCCESS, and underline the word.

**Aftercare** Keep the envelope in a business-type folder, file or other safe place until your business is up and running successfully. At this point, frame the photograph and display it on your desk, a wall or use it as a screensaver!

# to obtain a specific item

You are asking for something to come to you here, so a waxing Moon is essential. The day you choose should be relevant to the item you are seeking so consult the Table of Correspondences (see pages 18–19).

It's important that your goals in magic are honest and realistic, particularly when you are concentrating on material gain. Always, therefore, base your requests on genuine need, and don't be tempted by greed! In short, this is not a spell to use if you are hankering after a fancy new car or a designer coat.

Before having recourse to magic, try to assess whether you can attain the object of your desire by making a purchase or exchanging it for something already in your possession. If your need is genuine, and the item is beyond your current means, then it is time to use this spell. But don't abandon your budgeting and saving – magic helps those who help themselves! If you are the type of person whose efforts to save are often sabotaged by other priorities, this is a very useful spell indeed.

In the tradition of sympathetic magic, by caring for the bulb as it develops into a healthy plant, you will also be encouraging your wish to come true.

**You will need...**
- 1 green candle, or a white candle with the symbol for Earth inscribed on it (see pages 18–19)
- 1 flowering bulb in season, for either indoor or outdoor planting
- 1 flowerpot, approximately 10 cm in diameter
- Sufficient potting compost to fill the flowerpot
- 1 wineglass of water

# flower-bulb spell

Some bulbs need preparation prior to planting, so be sure to consult any instructions that come with the one you choose. The choice of an outdoor flowering plant does not necessarily mean casting the spell outside. It will work just as well indoors as out.

Visualize a circle of green light all around the area in which you will be working.

Light the candle, saying: '**Element of Earth whose gift is the material world, Witness and bless my request for** [item]. **May this manifest as this bulb grows and flowers**'.

Now take the bulb in both hands. Charge it with your request by chanting for at least three minutes the following words: '**Let the** [item] **come to me, As I will it, so mote it be!**'

Now that the bulb is 'en-chanted', fill the flowerpot with compost and plant the bulb according to its instructions.

Once it is planted, pour the wineglass of water onto the soil around it and allow to soak in.

**Aftercare** Follow instructions on the bulb pack regarding watering, feeding, position and so on in order to ensure that your bulb grows and flourishes. By the time it flowers, the item you have wished for should have appeared.

# to secure a holiday

If possible, cast this spell on a waxing Moon, as you are asking for an opportunity to come towards you. Sunday is luckiest, the traditional western day of rest from work, and ruled by the Sun, which oversees matters of well-being.

**You will need...**
1 slice wholemeal or wheatmeal bread, home-made or shop-bought
1 clean glass jar
1 plain tea light
1 sharp bread-knife

The word for holiday is originally derived from the term 'Holy Day'. This is because, before the Industrial Revolution, rural labour was shaped by the celebration of numerous saints' days that freed workers temporarily from the obligation of working for the benefit of the local lord. It is quite a useful term for this spell, as you can 'take a holiday' in all sorts of ways, some of which do not necessarily entail a two-week long stint abroad.

This spell is really about getting a break from the everyday obligation to study or work. It really does require an amount of trust in what you receive back from the request you are sending out into the ether; with magic, you tend to get what you need rather than what you think you want. This spell has been known to work in mysterious ways, so be prepared for anything!

# bread spell

This spell needs to be cast near a sea shore or by running water. Make sure that you are not contravening any local laws by carrying a bread-knife in a public place; a police cell is not the ideal place to spend a holiday!

Light the candle, put it in the glass jar and place it on the ground near the water's edge.

Hold up the bread towards the sun and say: **'I ask for the nourishment that comes from rest, May it come to me in the way that is best'.**

Cut the slice of bread into four equal pieces. Take one piece and hold it up, saying: **'I cast my wish to Air, that it be carried swiftly'**, then crumble it and scatter it for the birds to eat.

Take another piece and toast it over the candle saying: **'I cast my wish to Fire, that it shall be as I will'** and leave it for the birds.

Take the third piece and bury it in soil or sand, saying: **'I cast my wish to Earth, that it materialize'.**

Hold up the final piece towards the water saying: **'I cast my wish to Water, that it return on the tide'.**

Finish by saying: **'Spirit grant that it be so',** and blow out the candle.

**Aftercare** Remove the bread-knife, candle and jar and leave the five elements to dispose of the bread. Wait for your holiday to materialize.

# to successfully borrow money

Cast this charm on a waxing Moon, as you are aiming to increase your income by attracting the right sort of loan. Perform, if possible, on Thursday, day of Jupiter, which oversees matters of property and generosity.

There are times when we all need a bit of help in the financial department – whether we are trying to persuade reluctant parents to increase our allowance, supplementing our meagre student income with part-time work or starting out with a partner to set up home. This spell is designed to get a potential lender to look favourably upon your request.

As always, you need to be firmly grounded around material matters before you bring magic into play. In the case of finance, you should have a sensible repayment plan worked out before you approach your parents or bank manager.

Our aim is to draw the attention of the lender-to-be to your trustworthiness, reliability and the fact that you have a realistic grasp of your financial situation. Some practical research and calculations are required, therefore, prior to casting this spell.

You will need...
1 purple candle, or a white one with symbol of Jupiter (see right) carved into it
1 gold-coloured coin, of any denomination
15-cm length of elastic, or a large rubber band
1 small nail
1 small hammer
½ glass red wine, or red fruit juice
1 slice of bread

# coin and elastic spell

**21** This spell needs to be cast in the room that contains the 'hearth' of your home. In most homes this is the fireplace, but as many places are centrally heated nowadays, you will need to find a focal point that you feel is the heart of your home.

Light the candle and say: **'Jupiter, patron of generosity and guardian of property, Look favourably upon my request for a loan from** [name of potential lender]**'**.

Take your coin and wrap the elastic or rubber band around it firmly, leaving a loop that it can hang by.

Drive the nail into an appropriate point over your 'hearth' and hang up the coin by the loop of elastic by which it is held.

Take the glass of wine or juice, and offer it up to the spirit of the hearth by spilling a little on the ground in front of the coin, then drink all but a sip, which should be left in the glass.

Eat half of the bread and place the other half in the wine or juice remaining in the glass.

**Aftercare** Let the candle burn out completely in a safe place. Take the glass outside as soon as possible, and pour its contents onto the earth. Leave the coin hanging by the 'hearth' until you have entirely repaid the loan.

# for good luck to come into your life

As this is a spell for positive change, it should take place on a waxing Moon, ideally early in its cycle. Thursday, presided over by the Goddess Fortuna, is the most auspicious day to cast it.

Charms and spells for good fortune have been associated with magic for as long as curses and love spells. This is a good luck spell with a difference; you don't have to cross anyone's palm with silver or buy 'lucky' heather, and you even get to eat some sweets!

People seek to encourage good luck for all sorts of reasons; not all of them good, pressing or reasonable. It is often noted that witches and magicians are not particularly rich, and this fact is used to ridicule their abilities with magic. Good fortune, as you will find as you learn to work within the web of magic, has little to do with amassing an excess of money. This spell, accordingly, is designed to ensure a turning of your own life-tide in relation to fortune. The symbol used here is that of the cup waiting to be filled – in ancient runic lore the rune known as 'peorth' represents a dice-cup, and so is associated with choice and the whims of fortune.

## You will need...
- 1 purple or deep blue candle, or a candle inscribed with the symbol of Jupiter (see above right)
- 3 sweets wrapped in foil
- 1 thumbnail-sized piece of blu tack or plasticine
- 1 saucer or small plate

# sweet paper spell

 Making the sweet-paper cups may need a little practise beforehand; you could always get your friends to help you eat sweets left over from your experiments – if there are any.

Light the candle, saying: **'Lady Fortuna, may the light of your blessing and good fortune bless my spell'.**

Unwrap the sweets and carefully flatten out the foil wrappings.

Place your index finger halfway across a square of foil, and wrap it around, to form a thimble-sized 'cup'.

Twist the 'stem' of the cup, leaving enough foil to flatten out into a base. You should be left with a chalice-shaped cup. Repeat this process with the other two squares of foil.

Use the blu-tack or plasticine in order to secure the bases of the cups to the saucer.

Hold your right hand above the cups, and chant these words three times: **'Turn wheel turn, Burn flame burn, Bad luck gone, Fortunes turn'.**

Hold each sweet above the flame of the candle, then eat it.

**Aftercare** Allow the candle to burn right down. Place the cups in a safe place until you notice your fortunes beginning to change for the better. When they do, wrap some sweets in the foil used to make the cups, and give to someone else in need of good luck.

# creating your own spells

The information and advice given in this book will provide you with all the necessary framework you need to explore magic further. If you use the Table of Correspondences, refer to the Introduction and carefully follow the advice given about the use of Moon phases, you have the basic ingredients of sympathetic magic at your fingertips. The principles of banishing and binding, attracting or increasing are all laid out and demonstrated throughout the features and spells in this book. If you read diligently, and cast some of the spells yourself, you will then be perfectly capable of constructing your own.

As this book illustrates, making magic can be a very practical affair. Household items, supplies from the local chemist, supermarket or DIY shop are all potential tools and ingredients. The crafting of spells requires only two things: a basic knowledge of the principles of sympathetic magic, and the creativity and imagination that comes from within. This book provides you with the first essential, and hopefully some of the spells will inspire you to cultivate the second.

If you are not ready to go the whole way and make an entirely new spell of your own, there is nothing wrong in adapting or tweaking some of those provided between the covers of this book. If you are feeling adventurous, however, and wish to put together a spell all your own armed with your new-found knowledge, a strong sense of ethics and a pioneering spirit, there are other ways in which you can prepare for this.

One way is to get to know the elements intimately. You can do this by meditating on one at a time, thinking about their importance in our everyday, physical lives, and then actually getting out and experiencing them. You can also work at finding different ways of symbolizing or representing them in a way that is meaningful to you and your particular situation. The element of Fire, for example, will have very different connotations to someone living in a cold climate than it will to someone living on the edge of a volcano.

Another method of learning about magic is to try putting together spells using hypothetical case studies. The exercise below is intended to help you practise constructing a spell from scratch.

## exercise

The problem – a friend asks you to cast a spell for them as she is feeling depressed. Gentle but insistent questioning reveals that she is down because she has feelings for someone who doesn't know that she exists. Having revealed this, she asks for a love spell to make him notice her. What sort of spell do you think you should go for?

Possible answers will obviously depend on what you are hearing. On the one hand, the fact that she is feeling down tends to signal that she may need some gentle counselling and healing. On the other hand, if the bad feelings she is experiencing centre specifically on her desire for someone who doesn't pay her any attention, there may be an element of unhealthy fantasy at work. It could be that she simply needs a confidence boost.

If it is the first case, you would look at a healing spell and, if the second, a spell for self-confidence.

## the spell

Let us suppose that you need to design a healing spell. These are some of the questions you need to address:

- With which element do you think it is appropriate to work?
- At what phase of the Moon's cycle would it be best to work?
- Which day of the week is best suited to this spell?
- Which symbols could you use to represent your friend?
- What could you use to symbolize the depression?
- What would you do with these representations in order to enact healing?

## suggestions

The element of Water would be most suitable for this spell. As well as being concerned with healing, it also rules emotional and psychological issues.

If you are bringing about healing, choose a waxing Moon. If you decide upon a method by which you are going to be dismissing the depression, you will need to do so on a waning Moon for decrease. Monday, traditionally the day of the Moon, which is also associated with the emotions and psyche, would be best. For a guide to the phases of the Moon until 2008, turn to pages 124–5.

There are a range of possibilities here – you have the option of representing your friend in the shape of a person, perhaps with a doll or poppet, using wax, sewing materials or using an ice mould. Alternatively, you could use a symbol less obviously meant to be a person, such as a stone or a piece of fruit.

If you are going to represent your friend, the depression could be part of that symbol. For example, if you use an apple, you may name the peel as the illness, and peel it away as part of the spell, remove the pips and throw the remainder into a river or leave it in water for a few days. The pips, representing a new, recovered friend, can either be planted or given to your friend to eat. Alternatively, you may wish only to represent the depression itself. This could be a grape in an ice-cube, left in the sun to melt then wizen and prune, or a water-soaked sponge dried out over a radiator.

As you can see, there is never one set way of doing sympathetic magic and the range of possibilities also varies with each individual. It takes experience to find the best way of working, and the more you practise, the better you will get at identifying what is needed in individual cases.

Crafting spells can be engrossing, amazing and exciting. Whatever it means to you, one thing is guaranteed – long after crafting and casting spells becomes second nature, you will still find many things to wonder at and be surprised by.

Now that you have reached the end of this book, I offer you two spells – one for guidance on your path and one to bless you when you set out on it. All that remains for me to say, in the way of those who have chosen the path of magic, is:

Blessed Be.

# for guidance in life

Ideally, this spell should be cast at dark (new) Moon, when all things are possible. Any day is fine, but wait until after sundown to enact the ritual.

Designed to help you along your magical and life path, this spell is essentially a request for guidance in both. The phrase 'at a crossroads' is often used to describe a time of choosing the right direction in our lives. Here, the spell uses the magical traditions also associated with crossroads to help you find your way.

## crossroads spell

If you are assured of privacy, you could cast this at a deserted crossroads. However, the guidance below is designed for an indoor spell.

Visualize a circle of purple light all around the area in which you are working. Light the candle, saying: **'Hecate, old woman and goddess of the Crossroads, Bless me with your wisdom'.**

Tie the sticks together with the thread, making a cross of equal arms-lengths. Hold it above the candle and say: **'Hecate, please bless this charm, And keep its holder from all harm'.**

**Aftercare** Place the cross under your pillow and keep a dream diary for a month, noting all the symbols and patterns of your dreams – your guidance should come through these.

**You will need...**
1 purple or black candle
2 sticks, approximately 8 cm each in length
15-cm length of black or red thread, string or narrow cord

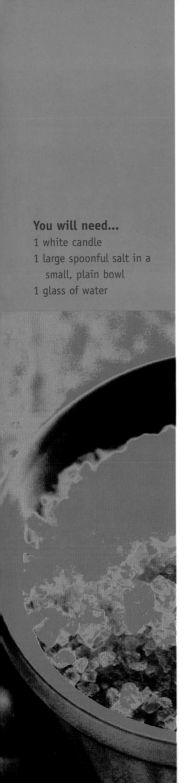

# for self-blessing

This is a spell used by witches when they feel in particular need of blessing or protection, and when they are about to embark on a new venture. It can be used whenever you feel in need of being blessed, slightly adrift from yourself or threatened. You can cast it at any time, according to your need.

**You will need...**
1 white candle
1 large spoonful salt in a
    small, plain bowl
1 glass of water

## salt and candle spell

You should bathe or shower before you cast this spell and remain completely naked for its duration.

Visualize a circle of dazzling white light all around the space in which you are working. Light the candle and take a step back.

Place a pinch of salt in the water, and sprinkle the remainder in front of you on the floor. Step onto the salt, carrying the salty water in the glass with you. Say aloud: **'I stand upon the good earth, and step into the light'.**

Anoint your feet, loins, chest, mouth and forehead with the salted water, saying at appropriate points: **'Bless my footsteps, Bless my loving, Bless my emotions, Bless my words, Bless my thoughts'.**

**Aftercare** You can remain within this circle for as long as you wish. Allow the candle to burn completely down in a safe place and vacuum or sweep up the salt after. Blessed Be!

# lunar calendar

This calendar will help you plan ahead and choose the correct phase of the Moon for casting spells. The half Moons on the charts mark the half-way points of the waxing and waning periods between dark and full Moon.

## 2001

| | ◐ | ○ | ◑ | ● |
|---|---|---|---|---|
| January | 2 | 9 | 16 | 24 |
| February | 1 | 8 | 15 | 23 |
| March | 3 | 9 | 16 | 25 |
| April | 1,30 | 8 | 15 | 23 |
| May | 29 | 7 | 15 | 23 |
| June | 28 | 6 | 14 | 21 |
| July | 27 | 5 | 13 | 20 |
| August | 25 | 4 | 12 | 19 |
| September | 24 | 2 | 10 | 17 |
| October | 24 | 2 | 10 | 16 |
| November | 22 | 1,30 | 8 | 15 |
| December | 22 | 30 | 7 | 14 |

## 2003

| | ◐ | ○ | ◑ | ● |
|---|---|---|---|---|
| January | 10 | 18 | 25 | 2 |
| February | 9 | 16 | 23 | 1 |
| March | 11 | 18 | 25 | 3 |
| April | 9 | 16 | 23 | 1 |
| May | 9 | 16 | 23 | 1,31 |
| June | 7 | 14 | 21 | 29 |
| July | 7 | 13 | 21 | 29 |
| August | 5 | 12 | 20 | 27 |
| September | 3 | 10 | 18 | 26 |
| October | 2 | 10 | 18 | 25 |
| November | 1,30 | 9 | 17 | 23 |
| December | 30 | 8 | 16 | 23 |

## 2002

| | | | | |
|---|---|---|---|---|
| January | 21 | 28 | 6 | 13 |
| February | 20 | 27 | 4 | 12 |
| March | 22 | 28 | 6 | 14 |
| April | 20 | 27 | 4 | 12 |
| May | 19 | 26 | 4 | 12 |
| June | 18 | 24 | 3 | 10 |
| July | 17 | 24 | 2 | 10 |
| August | 15 | 22 | 1,31 | 8 |
| September | 13 | 21 | 29 | 7 |
| October | 13 | 21 | 29 | 6 |
| November | 11 | 20 | 27 | 4 |
| December | 11 | 19 | 27 | 4 |

## 2004

| | | | | |
|---|---|---|---|---|
| January | 29 | 7 | 15 | 21 |
| February | 28 | 6 | 13 | 20 |
| March | 28 | 6 | 13 | 20 |
| April | 27 | 5 | 12 | 19 |
| May | 27 | 4 | 11 | 19 |
| June | 25 | 3 | 9 | 17 |
| July | 25 | 2,31 | 9 | 17 |
| August | 23 | 30 | 7 | 16 |
| September | 21 | 28 | 6 | 14 |
| October | 20 | 28 | 6 | 14 |
| November | 19 | 26 | 5 | 12 |
| December | 18 | 26 | 5 | 12 |

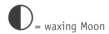 = waxing Moon  ◯ = full Moon   = waning Moon  ● = dark Moon

| 2005 | ◐ | ◯ | ◑ | ● |
|---|---|---|---|---|
| January | 17 | 25 | 3 | 10 |
| February | 15 | 24 | 2 | 8 |
| March | 17 | 25 | 3 | 10 |
| April | 16 | 24 | 2 | 8 |
| May | 16 | 23 | 1, 30 | 8 |
| June | 15 | 22 | 28 | 6 |
| July | 14 | 21 | 28 | 6 |
| August | 13 | 19 | 26 | 5 |
| September | 11 | 18 | 25 | 3 |
| October | 10 | 17 | 25 | 3 |
| November | 9 | 16 | 23 | 2 |
| December | 8 | 15 | 23 | 1, 31 |

| 2006 | | | | |
|---|---|---|---|---|
| January | 6 | 14 | 22 | 29 |
| February | 5 | 13 | 21 | 28 |
| March | 6 | 14 | 22 | 29 |
| April | 5 | 13 | 21 | 27 |
| May | 5 | 13 | 20 | 27 |
| June | 3 | 11 | 18 | 25 |
| July | 3 | 11 | 17 | 25 |
| August | 2, 31 | 9 | 16 | 23 |
| September | 30 | 7 | 14 | 22 |
| October | 29 | 7 | 14 | 22 |
| November | 28 | 5 | 12 | 20 |
| December | 27 | 5 | 12 | 20 |

| 2007 | ◐ | ◯ | ◑ | ● |
|---|---|---|---|---|
| January | 25 | 3 | 11 | 19 |
| February | 24 | 2 | 10 | 17 |
| March | 25 | 3 | 12 | 19 |
| April | 24 | 2 | 10 | 17 |
| May | 23 | 2 | 10 | 16 |
| June | 22 | 1, 30 | 8 | 15 |
| July | 22 | 30 | 7 | 14 |
| August | 20 | 28 | 5 | 12 |
| September | 19 | 26 | 4 | 11 |
| October | 19 | 26 | 3 | 11 |
| November | 17 | 24 | 1 | 9 |
| December | 17 | 24 | 1, 31 | 9 |

| 2008 | | | | |
|---|---|---|---|---|
| January | 15 | 22 | 30 | 8 |
| February | 14 | 21 | 29 | 7 |
| March | 14 | 21 | 29 | 7 |
| April | 12 | 20 | 28 | 6 |
| May | 12 | 20 | 28 | 5 |
| June | 10 | 18 | 26 | 3 |
| July | 10 | 18 | 25 | 3 |
| August | 8 | 16 | 24 | 1, 30 |
| September | 7 | 15 | 22 | 29 |
| October | 7 | 14 | 21 | 28 |
| November | 6 | 13 | 19 | 27 |
| December | 5 | 12 | 19 | 27 |

# index

# acknowledgements

I would like to thank everyone at Carroll & Brown and Penguin US who have supported this book, especially Rachel Aris and Charlotte Beech. Many thanks to my friend and agent, Liz Puttick, for her constant enthusiasm and encouraging words. To Jan Harper, Jayne Ovens and Cathy Lubelska, my circle friends and women of spirit – many cheers for inciting me to write about my magical experiences and helping me test-drive the spells over many years. Thanks to Ann and Heather of the Pink Teapot, for inviting me back year after year to run workshops on magic and witchcraft in the Women's Dome at the Big Green Gathering, and also to the women who participated. I would like to express my gratitude to my patient children, Michelle, Chantal and Matthew, and most of all, I would like to thank my wonderful partner, Steve, for his unswerving and unconditional support throughout this project.

**Production**
Karol Davies, Nigel Reed and Paul Stradling

**Carroll & Brown would like to thank the following:**
Ellen Parton
Megan Selmes

**Picture credit:**
page 100: David Murray